The Art of Expectations

A SIMPLE WAY TO PREDICT OUTCOMES USING EXPECTATIONS

Louis J Ebner III

The Art of Expectations
A Simple Way to Predict Outcomes Using Expectations
By Louis J Ebner III

Copyright © 2011 by Louis J Ebner III

Contents

Introduction

Our destination is unclear; the reasons we change direction is not. Quite simply, we are as predictable as animals that migrate from one destination to another or ones that choose to hibernate to avoid inclement weather. Where they migrate or hibernate may change, but the action is predictable. Our inclement weather that creates our predictable actions comes from expectations.

We will discuss how expectations are what really make the world go around. These expectations are what give us individual worth and purpose. We will learn that our expectations are measurable, therefore, making our actions predictable.

The majority of this book we will discuss how expectations make us predictable. We will establish human instincts and define them as "Attributes of Normal." We will discuss how our expectations are set and what influences them. We will also discuss the profound effect of groups on our expectations and actions.

To bring these concepts together in a usable tool we will discuss lastly a simple "Stock Market Expectations Indicator," which has proved very accurate in predicting market turns since its inception in 2009. This indicator takes the mystery out of the stock market and makes sense of its erratic actions.

I understand that it is in our nature to want to skip directly to the stock market indicator, but I would caution, it is important to understand why it works in order to use it correctly. The concepts and the indicator discussed in the following are a perspective on how we should view others and ourselves.

Disclaimer

The concepts and tools discussed in this book represent the opinion of the author and do not constitute any type of financial advice. All matters of your financial situation should be left to the financial professionals you employ.

1

What is Normal?

Your thoughts run wild with anticipation on the definition of normal. You are reading this just to prove that you do not have anything in common with what I classify as normal. Welcome to normal.

The thoughts and the inspirations we have are not the topic of this book. Even though I would argue they are probably pretty normal as well, this is a discussion of our predictable actions and reactions.

We acknowledge our similarities with our study of behaviorism. We take relief in identifying with someone else. Our behavioral similarities are just as predictable as a population of bears. We understand how bears respond when they're hungry and scared. We understand that bears hibernate in the winter. What we don't know is what they are thinking.

This book will focus on "Normal" as it pertains to who we are and why we do what we do. Our "Normal" is defined by our influences and instincts.

"Instinct puts us into the situation and influence determines our actions."

Instincts are normal, and no matter how we feel about a situation, more than likely, they will get the best of us. Expectations are what sets the bar for us personally and professionally and influences our reactions. Understanding who we are by defining "Normal" allows us to predict our actions.

1.1 The 7 Attributes of Normal

If we were all so different and random, then there would be no traffic in the world.

Normal is defined as conforming to a standard, being typical. Our thoughts and our dreams are random at best, but our actions and reactions are typical and conform to a standard. Not every person will conform to normal all the time, but the majority will and this makes the attributes of normal important to understand in predicting outcomes to events or actions. Every action has a reaction; these reactions can be as predictable as cornering a wild animal.

There are seven primary characteristics of "Normal" that play a large part in our typical reactions to events or actions. We classify these attributes of "Normal" as:

- Addictive Nature
- Selective Hearing
- Belief in Fairytales
- Special Complex
- Reluctantly Hopeful
- Risk Taker
- Need for Happiness

These attributes are not meant to define who we are as individuals. They are characteristics of our animal nature; therefore, they are our instincts. Bears hibernate for the winter, and humans have these characteristics. What the bear dreams about plays no role in their preparation for the winter. What dreams and fantasies we have play no role in our response to actions and events.

1.2 Our Addictive Personalities

Addiction is used very commonly referring to smokers, alcoholics, drug abusers, and gamblers. For the most part the word "addiction" carries a negative overtone.

The list of addictions or what is classified as one has grown over time. A smoker a generation ago was not an addict. An individual who drank more than three drinks a day was not an alcoholic a generation ago. The opium user two generations ago was not a drug addict. A perpetual losing gambler was not classified as an addict two generations ago.

Webster's Dictionary defines addiction as compulsive physiological need for and use of a habit-forming substance, such as heroin, nicotine, or alcohol, characterized by tolerance and by well-defined physiological symptoms upon withdrawal; broadly: persistent compulsive use of a substance known by the user to be physically, psychologically, or socially harmful. The American Heritage Dictionary includes another definition to the word addiction as the condition of being habitually or compulsively occupied with or involved in something. They actually even gave an example: addiction to fast cars. This addition to the definition allowed compulsive behaviors, such as gambling, to be classified as addictions. This also allowed other compulsive behaviors to be included, such as sex, violence, athleticism, diet, etc.

Almost every habit or ritual could be classified as some sort of addiction with The American Heritage Dictionary's further definition. After using the restroom most of us look to wash our hands. If we are unable to wash our hands, typically we will feel a slight anxiety over contaminates on our hands. Since we feel a form of anxiety over not being able to wash our hands, this would classify this habit as an addiction.

Most people's lives revolve around daily rituals and habits. If our daily ritual is to wake up and immediately brush our teeth, what happens if we don't have any toothpaste left? We will feel anxiety over our potential bad breath. Most habits and rituals can be labeled as addictions.

The medical community validates these classifications of addictions by labeling them as:

Positive Addiction – This addiction's benefits outweigh its negative ones.

Negative Addiction – This addiction's costs do no outweigh their reward.

Neutral Addiction – This addiction is unclear whether there is a positive or negative effect.

The medical community takes our addictive personalities and labels and classifies them. Today every twitch, bump and noise must have a label. Our addictions are just "normal."

When most of us think of a person with an addiction, we picture a drug addict in a back alleyway gazing into oblivion or an alcoholic passed out by the curb. This image of an addict is really just a person who has taken a common addiction to their limit. All addictions have a starting point. An action becomes an addiction (habit) when we no longer think about it. When we think about an action, it is not an addiction. Most of the addictions we have peak at some point. This peak of an addiction may or may not be harmful or socially unacceptable. A runner starts out by

7

running several miles. A runner will continue to run more and more until it hurts. Society believes running is healthful; therefore, this addiction is acceptable although this runner is hurting him or herself.

We all have habits and rituals; therefore, we have addictive personalities. Addiction is "normal."

1.3 The Fairytales We Live by

"I will go to the moon someday." This statement carries a sense of hope and possibilities to our children. That same statement carries a sense of regret as we age. When we are children, our dreams and hopes for the future create a magical land of potential. Age and society tend to take away this enlightened path of fairytales and dreams. What makes these realities harder to accept is that at one point in our lives it was possible to achieve.

Nothing in life comes easy. Fairytales tell us of a place where life is simpler and full of hope. The saying "life is cruel" has been proven more true over time then these stories and dreamlands we create in our minds. This is not a pessimistic view on life; it is just a view in the mirror, a face to what is real.

Our beliefs in these fairytales smooth out the sharp edges of life. It is another form of self-preservation. Our dreams allow us to look past the bleak present and dream of better days.

Most dreams and fairytales we create as children focus on what we want to be when we grow up. When we become adults, this fairytale world becomes less about our distant futures and more about what is right around the corner.

There comes a time in our lives when our dreams of the future, the way we imagined our lives would be, fail. This realization of our current lives to what we thought they should be can manifest differently in people. The most obvious sign that a person is facing this perceived failure is change. Some common outcomes to this realization are: divorce, midlife crisis, career change, relocation, and sometimes, unfortunately, suicide.

Some people achieve their dreams from childhood. Sometimes when we achieve a dream it is not what we expected. This letdown can create similar reactions to not achieving our dreams. "We are damned if we do and damned if we don't."

Without hopes and dreams what is there to live for? We need these dreams and fairytales to get through the years. This makes them "Normal."

1.4 We Only Hear What We Want to Hear

How many times during a disagreement or altercation with another family member or friend have we been told that we only listen to what we want to hear or we have "selective hearing." All human beings have "selective hearing." This condition is a form of self-protection. In extreme cold our body will begin to shiver to create friction to heat us. When we are being overwhelmed with information that is causing us unnecessary duress, our minds choose to ignore or overlook this potentially important information.

Just as an individual person suffers from this condition so do large groups of people. Groups tend to delude themselves for a longer period of time than a person who is not a member.

Like an individual person, groups tend to have "selective hearing" on topics that threaten their "Normal" lives. Before 9/11, we were aware of terrorists; but we chose not to pay attention to the warning signs because we chose not to hear them. If there is no event, then our "selective hearing" (delusion) will continue.

How many years after Christopher Columbus discovered America, proving the world was not flat, did people still harbor the fear of falling off the edge of the earth. I will wager that it took a generation or two to dismiss the fear entirely. New discoveries or disproven truths tend to last a generation, at least, because these disproven facts are almost like a scar on our memories. History has shown us delusions can last for hundreds and thousands of years. One thing is for sure – we will know when the end of the world is coming, but we will likely choose not to see or hear it.

We all have selective hearing. Selective hearing is "Normal."

1.5 How Special We Think We Are

When the psychologist refers to someone with a superiority complex, they will immediately compare them to someone with an inferiority complex. A person with a superiority complex has high expectations for themselves while someone with an inferiority complex has low expectations. This common definition of a superiority complex is not an attribute to normal; it is just a stage in a person's constant swing between high and low expectations. A person could suffer from a superiority complex one day and then inferiority the next.

This attribute of "normal" is how we feel different and special from others, which results in naming it the special complex. The underlying attributes of the special complex are similarly used to describe someone with a superiority complex, defined as an exaggerated opinion of one's worth and abilities. The difference is that a person's belief in how special they are never changes. The special complex is our belief that we are one of a kind, our thoughts and dreams make us different. When we are riding high on success, we credit our personal effort that brought us the achievement. When we have a streak of bad luck, we look to blame someone or something else. If we blamed all of our failures entirely on ourselves, we would have to assume we knew better. It is hard for us to imagine that we could not have helped ourselves. Failure is harder to accept if we are to blame.

The special complex is a form of narcissism but with the lack of physical vanity. It is the image we have of ourselves and how we impact others. We never truly know how we impact others. Since all we know is how we perceive them and not how others do, it is impossible for us to truly understand our impact on other people. Empathy is our attempt to relate to other people, but our special complex trumps this influence.

The special complex is our view of the world. It is a form of self-preservation since it makes us feel special. Life would be rather dismal if we did not find ourselves interesting.

This perception of our self-worth is a primary attribute of "Normal." We all feel special; therefore, it is "Normal."

1.6 Reluctantly Hopeful

After the technology stock crash of the early 2000s, America and the world focused their energy and funds toward real estate. In the beginning the growth was fueled by low interest rates and easier credit terms. It also was a better place to put money that we would have otherwise put into the stock market that was out of favor.

The technology bust woes were quickly replaced with the American dream. After several years of prosperity, the real estate market hit the mainstream. This booming market was not a secret. Most of the population of America knew that real estate prices were climbing fast. What kept the general public from immediately joining this market was reluctance and fear. Not until many more pass are we willing to make the trek on our own, which is a common characteristic of a herding animal. We look for leaders to lead us in new directions.

The real estate values in some areas nearly doubled in several years. Everyone was looking at real estate. Real estate flipping reality television shows dominated the airways. People bought properties that they clearly could not afford since they felt they could sell it in a year or less for a profit.

The real estate market peaked and started to slide. We are now hopeful that it will come back. Real estate professionals and political powers are telling us that there is value in real estate. They are hopeful that we can get back to normal.

Charles Dow had theorized in his editorials, in the Wall Street Journal, that the stock market moved in stages. Most technical analysts strictly focus on the price movements, but Charles Dow had reasons for these movements.

Dow believed the first general market move up was the bargain hunters who identified an undervalued market. The market would then sell off some of the gain as some of the bargain hunters left the market looking for other bargains. Having made a strong move higher, the market is no longer a secret, and general investors push the market even higher based on current growth and present profitability. Once the market has been saturated with general investors growth in the value of that market is slowed, and it will begin to shrink. Dreamers drive the last move higher. The last movement pushes well above its true or future value, typically driven by the main street investors, the general public. When the market is in this stage, it is erratic and volatile. The market is erratic since the general public is unaware of what its value is; they are just playing the lottery. Volume starts to diminish since the market is running out of investors. Everyone who could or would invest has already done so.

After these three stages are up, the market moves down in a similar fashion. The first leg down is driven by profit taken from a stalling market. Then the market will attempt to recover unsuccessfully. This first recovery attempt is typically driven by the main street that missed the last move higher. Then the market will sell off again; typically, this move down is the largest move. Selling in this leg down is driven by validated fear; rumors become reality. The market is falling on reduced growth and over capacity. Following this move down, the market will attempt to bounce again on fair market valuations again unsuccessfully. This last move down is investors surrendering; Main Street is getting out at the ground floor. Even though the market is fairly valued, too many dreams have been shattered, and the thought of owning stock in this market makes the general public sick. Lastly, the market finds a bottom, and this is where the bargain hunters start the cycle over again.

The (Charles) Dow Theory was used with surprising success by William Hamilton from 1902 to 1929 when he predicted all but one market movement in the Wall Street Journal editorials he wrote. William Hamilton, using Charles Dow's theory, predicted the stock market crash of 1929. He died just months before the crash. William Hamilton wrote a book called "The Stock Market Barometer" in 1922. Robert Rhea wrote "The Dow Theory" in 1932 clarifying William Hamilton's book. "The Dow Theory" text is actually only the first third of the book; the remaining two thirds are reprints of William Hamilton's editorials from the Wall Street Journal.

The Dow Theory is used by many technical stock market analysts today. Unfortunately, the human behavioral reasons for the market moves are neglected. This oversight is probably why William Hamilton's success has not been duplicated.

Main Street is always last to enter a market because of our reluctance and need for validation. Once on board, Main Street typically suffers the most because of our hope for normalcy. Hope is really just our unwillingness to let go of the past.

These typical behaviors are very "Normal." We are reluctant on the way up and hopeful on the way down.

1.7 The Risk Taker in All of Us

The word risk commands different emotions from different people. The Heritage dictionary defines risk as:

- The possibility of suffering harm or loss; danger.

- A factor, thing, element, or course involving uncertain danger; a hazard.

Many of us associate risk immediately to the loss of money or danger to ourselves. By definition, risk is much more than just losing money or harming ourselves. Risk is on both sides over every action and event.

If we are unwilling to accept risk on investments, we risk not gaining on those investments. If we never risk injury, than we will be unable to eat, sleep or drink, since all these actions carry some sort of risk. If we never took any risk on relationships, then we would be risking being alone.

Whether we know it or not, we accept risk every day. The risks we take may be in attempting to limit risk itself. We all take risks and to some the possibility of gain trumps the possible loss; to others it is the opposite. A person willing to accept harm or loss for gain takes just as much risk as the person who is not.

From 1839 to 1843, 1873 to 1879, and 1929 to 1932 the United States suffered economic depressions. These American Depressions were the result of credit defaults, failed banks and deflation. Taking too much risk caused each depression. History tells us that too much credit risk eventually leads to a depression, but the unwillingness to accept risk again prolongs their effects. Time and time again we continue to repeat the errors of our forefathers.

Each depression approximately occurred in a span of a life expectancy (at the time) away from each other. From this correlation alone, it is fair to say, it only takes us to a generation to forget. Once we forget, our instincts take over, and we repeat history all over again.

Risk is present throughout history. The risks we take are generally no different than the ones our forefathers took. History tells us that our instincts determine the risks we take since we continue to repeat the errors of the past. There is no life without risk. Even by never leaving our homes we take risks. The only way to avoid all risk is to not be born. To be a risk taker is absolutely "Normal."

1.8 Our Eternal Search for Happiness

The glass is always half full; if we believe otherwise, then we are pessimists. This way of thinking comes from our belief that positive thoughts bring us positive outcomes. We need positive thoughts in order to achieve happiness. Unfortunately, life is never so simple. A glass half full can make a bad situation worse.

Our need to be happy combined with our reluctantly hopeful attributes can compound situations. The reason markets tumble when bubbles burst is because of how long we ignore the signs (selective hearing). A market bubble swells well above demand to create an unrealistic market. As soon as the market runs out of buyers it collapses on itself.

Another term for this positive feeling is euphoria. When we perceive ourselves as being happy, we become euphoric. We will search our entire lives for happiness. We experience times of euphoria followed by similar extremes of depression. Expectations play a large role in where we are in our cycle of happiness and depression,, which we will discuss at length later.

Some individuals use artificial means to simulate this feeling with drugs and alcohol. When we combine our addictive nature with a need for happiness, abuse of these stimulants becomes common.

Many countries banned short selling in the recent financial crisis. A bank's stock price plays a role in their leverage requirements by the Federal Deposit Insurance Corporation. When their leverage goes below the required level, they are threatened with takeover by the FDIC. Since short sellers are hoping the value of a stock goes down, their activities can threaten a bank's leverage requirements. Some referred to short sellers as unpatriotic. When investors buy bank stocks, it gives banks more leverage to lend. The cause of the credit crisis was not a lack of credit but an over extension of it. Short sellers did not cause the credit crisis, but interestingly, they were the only ones reprimanded during this event.

If the short sellers win over the reluctant and make them hopeful, then they will be the new meaning of happiness; and the buyers will be the pessimists.

Man has such a requirement for happiness that we hate those who threaten it. We all search for happiness; and this is why it is an attribute of "Normal."

1.9 The Select Few–The Abnormal

When we describe ourselves as different and unique, we fail to recognize that our similarities outweigh our differences. A normal human being has two eyes, one nose, one mouth, two ears, two hands, 10 fingers, two arms, two legs, 10 toes, etc. Although we see ourselves as different, I would wager that a bear only sees us as human, just another animal in the woods. After all, a bear is a bear, and a human is a human. If a bear is born with three legs rather than four, they still have the instinct to hibernate. Physical abnormalities do not affect our actions and decisions. If we are born with one arm, this physical abnormality does not affect our "Normal" attributes. If a bear went south for the winter instead of hibernating, this would be abnormal.

Abnormal behavior is not the lack of one or more of the seven attributes of "Normal" rather an extreme of one or more. The bear who goes south for the winter is likely pushing the limits of one or more of their instincts then missing one. If a person washes their hand 12 times each time they use the rest room, their extreme addiction to washing their hands makes them abnormal.

If a person pushes their risk attribute above normal limits, they would be classified as abnormal. An extreme sports participant is pushing their risk of death while the person suffering from Agoraphobia is pushing their risk of not living a normal life.

A "Normal" person feels pity, fear or admiration for an abnormal individual. An abnormal person will stand out from the rest. The actions of an abnormal individual affect the emotions of a "Normal" person. When we are faced with abnormalities, immediately we compare ourselves to them. If we perceive this person to be inferior to us, then we will take pity. If we feel this person is superior, we will admire them. From the above example, we would likely admire the extreme sports participant and take pity on the Agoraphobic person.

Sometimes an abnormal behavior makes us feel fear. This comes from our inability to relate to the abnormality. For example, a serial killer who is pushing their need for happiness to an abnormal extreme does not command admiration or pity but instead creates fear in a "Normal" person who cannot relate to this extreme for happiness.

Whether we pity the compulsive hand washer or fear the mass murderer, these emotions are caused by the extreme actions of abnormal people. Actions are what define abnormalities. Our thoughts of abnormal behavior are common. We may dream about exhibiting abnormal behavior, but without action, these fantasies are "Normal."

The Art of Expectations

2

The Normal Group Mentality

"An individual in a crowd is a grain of sand amid other grains of sand, which the wind stirs up at will."

Gustave Le Bon – The Crowd 1896

A person's attributes of "Normal" are self-balancing. Unless abnormal, our "Normal" attributes may push to limits but will not go beyond a socially acceptable threshold. If we are a part of a group, these thresholds can be broken.

Since a group of individuals are capable of pushing beyond normal limits, this makes groups abnormal. If we are not a part of a group, their actions will command the same emotions as abnormal people do. We will pity, fear or admire them. Depending on how we relate to the group's actions will determine our emotional response.

During World War II many Germans committed horrific acts while under the influence of the Nazi group. The Nazis believed they were special. They believed their race was superior and therefore, gave them the right to abolish those who they felt were inferior. After the war many of the actions of the Nazis were punished, but many were not. The soldiers who committed these actions would not have done them on their own. It took a group to push them beyond a normal threshold.

In 1896 Gustave Le Bon published his book "The Crowd – A Study of the Popular Mind." This publication is one of the most ground-breaking studies in Group Psychology. Mussolini was said to have a copy of the Bible and this book on his night stand during World War II.

"The crowd is always intellectually inferior to the isolated individual."

Gustave Le Bon – The Crowd

The findings of Gustave Le Bon are still true today as they were thousands of years before he wrote of them. When a person is under the influence of a crowd, they will revert to their primitive instincts and break socially acceptable normal barriers. The actions of a group can be either heroic or destructive.

During war soldiers go beyond normal thresholds in defending the beliefs of their group. A soldier will remember a war; when it is over, he will go back to his life before the war. Depending on what side of the war we are on will determine how we view his actions as either heroic or destructive. The actions of the German soldiers as described above were destructive, although they believed they were being heroic.

A group mentality does not necessarily just include acts of violence. To be a member of a group means that we are being influenced by that group. If we are an American, then we are a member of the United States of America. If we invest in stocks, then we are shareholders.

2.1 Group Influence

Gustave Le Bon gave three common characteristics of a person who is a member of a group.

- Feeling Invincible – Members will feel that they are impervious to harm. This characteristic is what allows people to break their normal thresholds.

- Contagion – The actions of groups are contagious. A person who admires the acts of a group will feel enticed to join them.

- Under a Hypnotic Spell – Once a member, he or she is hypnotized by the group's influence. They will no longer be in control of their actions.

Whether we join a group or not, has a lot to do with who and where we are from. A group's influence will have little affect if we do not admire their actions. If we pity or fear the actions of the group, their influence is powerless over us.

A group's influence over us is born out of our admiration for their actions. Admiration is the result of a quality we wish we possess.

Legends can command admiration as well. A legendary action may be all that is needed to form a group. Legends are not just mythical men or women who performed superhuman acts. During the California Gold rush it was the legend of a huge gold strike that enticed men and women to pack up and take a life-threatening journey to California. This journey is an example of a group taking abnormal risk. The prospectors of the California Gold Rush were part of a group.

Inherited group memberships can have a large influence over us. When we are born, it is likely we are already a member of several groups. If we come from a devout Catholic family, we are members of the Catholic Church at birth. Even if we chose to leave that group later in life, the exposure will influence our admiration of religious groups. A group membership at birth can include citizenship, social class, gender, and even birth defects. If we are born blind, then we will likely feel admiration towards a group who is fighting for more access for the blind.

The community we are raised in will influence our feeling of admiration for groups as well. If we are raised in an oppressive country where freedom is limited, groups created by legendary freedom fighters will more than likely command our admiration.

As human beings we have common influences. These influences, no matter where we are from, will command some sort of admiration. The two most common are greed and fear. Since these feelings are prevalent in so many people, groups that command this type of influence typically have large memberships. Both greed and fear have created some of the most destructive and constructive groups over time.

It is normal for human beings to join and participate in group actions. We are all hopeful, and this attribute combined with our need for happiness will make us seek out groups that command our admiration. Because we are drawn to groups by our "Normal" Attributes, membership is therefore "Normal." It could also be said that normalcy leads to

29

abnormal behavior. This conclusion makes the outcome to abnormal acts predictable.

2.2 Group Leaders

"In every social sphere, from the highest to the lowest, as soon as a man ceases to be isolated he speedily falls under the influence of a leader."

Gustave Le Bon – The Crowd

A real leader is not a person who merely is looking for power. A leader is the greatest believer in the acts committed by the group they form.

The world is full of people who are seeking power over others. This person is typically under the influence of a group whose admiration is controlled by greed. A person who seeks power under the influence of greed typically attempts to gain it by fear. Greed and fear have a relationship which can motivate many individuals. Power achieved by fear will not create a group of individuals willing to follow that leader to the ends of the earth. The fear can actually create the opposite effect. Groups can be formed to topple the greed-driven leader. Fear and tyranny can create legends of freedom fighters. A leader who takes their strength from greed will not go down in history as a hero but rather the opposite. Legends are created by abnormal acts.

There are two types of leaders who can motivate a group of individuals to perform abnormal acts.

A leader in the moment is an individual who becomes stimulated by an event or action. This leader can topple governments or win unwinnable battles in a war. This individual is already part of a larger group and is acting within the parameters of their higher power. A leader of the moment, power fades as the moment passes.

The most rare and remembered leader is self-motivated. This leader will sacrifice everything for their ideals. Group actions start with its leaders, and they are the strongest force behind the act. A rare leader, as described above, leaves their mark on society in the history books. A rare leader is able to perform abnormal acts without the influence of a group. They are born with the ability to perform abnormal acts.

Martin Luther King motivated and continues to motivate millions of individuals even after his death. He sacrificed everything for his ideals. His abnormal need for happiness captured the imaginations of millions. This image of freedom he projected was so powerful that he has become a founding father of equality in the United States.

Jim Jones is best known for leading over 900 individuals in a mass suicide. His abnormal need for happiness influenced the control over his members to such a degree that they took their own lives at his command. Surviving members still are unable to explain how the event that led to this mass suicide unfolded.

"When under the influence of a powerful leader, we are merely deer in headlights."

2.3 Weak Leaders

When an individual is part of a group driven by a strong leader with great conviction, their actions and mentality exhibits abnormal behavior. The opposite holds true with groups led by weak leaders driven by selfish intentions. A group that is led by false pretenses exhibits normal behaviors.

This opposite effect of a weak leader is due to the lack of real influence. A person becomes a member of a group led by a weak leader because of previous experiences they had from another group with similar intentions that was lead by a strong leader. A person's membership in this new group, led by a weak leader, is a testament to the power and influence a strong leader leaves on its members.

A perfect example of weak leadership exists in party politics. In the United States there are two predominate parties that divide the nation. If we are a member of either the Democratic or Republican Party, at one point in our past a strong leader of this group captured our admiration. It is also possible that our membership could be the result of our membership in another group who supports this party. It is rare in today's politics to have a strong leader in control of a political party.

Most political parties are lead by leaders with selfish intent, and therefore, the influence over the group members is weak. The membership is more social, and the behaviors and actions of these groups are normal. A member of a group with a weak leader will not follow that leader into battle. Weak leaders stand on the shoulders of giants.

2.4 Dramatic Change to Normal Group Behavior

We have all heard the expression "life is full of surprises." This expression is more sarcasm than wisdom. Life is actually full of a lot of the same, with very few surprises. These "surprises," as referred to in the expression, are actually just unlikely but possible outcomes.

If we play the lottery and win, are we actually surprised? Winning was always a possible outcome although rare. So winning is not really an unexpected outcome, just an extraordinary one. We play the lottery to win, so it should be no surprise to win. If we lose, we will still probably continue to play the lottery.

If we won the lottery and the agency said they were bankrupt and unable to pay, this would be a surprise. This surprise would probably stop us from playing the lottery again.

Real "surprises" are outcomes that we could not have anticipated. These unique and unimaginable outcomes force change.

The stock market going up or down 5 percent, 10 percent, 20 percent, or 90 percent is a possible outcome and should be no surprise. Our stock broker running a Ponzi scheme and stealing our money is a surprise. In "Fortune's Formula" written by William Poundstone, he described Kelly's Criteria for betting that if we continue to bet where zero is one of the possible outcomes, then eventually we will end up with zero. If all of our money is invested in stocks, then it should be no surprise if our account becomes worthless one day, since that is a possible outcome of stocks (bankruptcy). We diversify to avoid this zero outcome.

On August 8, 1904, the Dow Jones Industrial Average closed at 53. Twenty-five years later on August 26, 1929, the Dow Jones Industrial Average had risen nearly seven fold to close at 380.33. On July 8, 1932, the Dow closed at 41.22. If the stock market is just a meter to the willingness to accept risk, was the stock market collapse the "surprise" or was it the unthinkable banking system collapse that occurred at the same time. People had less money to put into banks and defaulted on debt which created a high demand on the dollar which led to less lending. This series of events started the deflationary spiral which pushed unemployment in America to record levels. The stock market went down because people stopped playing the lottery.

It took the Dow 25 years to get back to even. In November 1954 the Dow Jones Industrial Average finally reached the 1929 levels. After another 25 years, in 1979, the Dow Jones Industrial Average reached the low 800s. So, it would have taken a lifetime to double the Dow Jones Industrial Average from August 26, 1929.

Real "surprises" take a long time to forget. It typically takes a generation to forget these life-changing events. The market nearly went up 12 fold 25 years later. In November 2004, the Dow reached 10,500. The Great Depression appears to have taken a generation to forget.

The Great Depression has occurred in other countries and other times over and over again. No real surprises can change the human condition. Risk is an instinct and not a choice.

The Art of Expectations

3

Why We Do What We Do

Our lives revolve around very simple feelings. These feelings can be described as despair and euphoria. When our expectations are high, we are euphoric yet react with despair. When we have low expectations, we live in despair yet react euphorically. This cycle of reactions helps explain why we do what we do.

Expectations are simply the neutral line between a positive and negative effect. When we have high expectations, we tend to focus on the negative. When we have low expectations, we tend to focus on the positive. This relationship between being and reacting create an ongoing effect that cycle from one extreme to the next. Someone who has high expectations will eventually have low expectations and vice versa.

This process of moving from one state of expectations to another defines our lives in the choices we make, the paths we take. Most expectations are set even before we are born. If we are born in Japan, we are expected to speak Japanese.

Failure to meet this primary expectation will change the course of our life.

From the second we are conceived, expectations begin to be set for us. Before a newborn leaves the hospital, their lives already have a long list of expectations to live up to.

3.1 The Decisions We Make

The decisions we make are not based on just the moment we make them. The decisions we make are based on current and previous expectations met, exceeded or missed.

If faced with a decision of whether to have steak or fish, our previous expectations will determine our response. If our last order of fish missed our expectations, then we will likely order steak.

If a neighbor of ours recently died of mad cow disease and they ate regularly at the restaurant we are ordering from, this "surprise" would cause us to choose the fish. Although we have been aware of mad cow disease for many years, only until our neighbor died of it did we choose to pay attention to the dangers of it.

When we take a new job, we believe that the "grass is greener" in that pasture. Our "Normal" attributes have us fantasize how much better tomorrow could be and influence our decisions we make today. How else could we decide to leave what we know for the unknown without fantasies?

Small decisions can be attributed to large events. Likewise large decisions can be influenced by small events. The decisions we make are really not ours to make. Our responses are already determined. The situation just needs to present itself.

All expectations are influenced by our seven instinctual attributes of "Normal." The actions we take are, therefore, "Normal."

Most of our decisions we make come back to our "Normal" need for happiness. We have dreams, hopes and reluctance; feel special; are deluded; and take risks so we can be happy.

3.2 What are Expectations

Expectations, as mentioned previously, are a person's line between a positive or negative reaction to actions or events. When we travel on a road in a car our goal is to stay within the lines. These lines do not determine whether we are going north or south, but they are the lines that manage to keep us alive during our journey from point A to B.

Expectations lines are drawn by the world we live in. If we are born into a religious family who has a long history of entering into law enforcement, then your religious and career expectations are more than likely already defined. It is almost impossible for a person to be born without any expectations. Expectations give us meaning and purpose. If we have no expectations, then we have no reason to get out of bed or in it for that matter.

Unfortunately, our normal attributes perpetuate our recurring cycle from high to low expectations. Utopia should be defined as a world where expectations are always perfectly met. If expectations were perfect, then there would be no great moments in time as well as terrible ones. With the good comes the bad. We are always on a road of expectations; whether it is on a path of high or low the outcomes are always the same.

If we are on a path of high expectations, we are being motivated and driven by the feelings they produce. As discussed earlier, while we are in an ascending expectations cycle our overall expectations are low, which means we look for the negative over the positive. This perception leads us to be surprised by the positives. There are many words to describe this feeling a person experiences in the beginning of building high expectations such as reluctant, hesitant, cautious, tentative, or doubtful. The higher we ascend in expectations the more intense our feelings become. Some words that describe these more intense feelings are euphoric, exhilarated, excited, ecstatic, or blissful. Our feelings turn from reluctance to acceptance of our situation.

As expectations build in a person, so does their confidence. Higher and higher a person climbs in exceeding expectations, the more confident they are in their decisions, and therefore, they will be more hopeful as they begin to miss expectations.

When high expectations peak, then opposite feelings will start to develop. As discussed earlier, when we begin a descending expectations cycle we have high expectations and will focus on the positive over the negative. This perception leads us to be surprised by the negatives. These feelings can be described as hopeful, encouraged, positive, optimistic, or expectant. Our feelings of high expectations are a normal response to our hopeful nature. High expectations are signaled by a feeling of hope gradually turning to despair. The lower our expectations go the more intense the feelings become. Some words to describe these growing feelings of lowering expectations are cynical, depressed, disheartened, discouraged, and unhappy.

The lowering of a person's expectations typically takes less time than the building of them. The process of lowering expectations eventually leads us to feel reluctant. As a person's expectations are lowered, so are their confidence and self-assurance. When their expectations hit bottom, the process will repeat by building expectations all over again.

This cycle of expectations can exist in multiple stages with different expectations a person is dealing with. As in a previous example, the person born into a religious, law enforcement family may be content with religion but discouraged with their law enforcement career path. When a person's expectations cycles are coordinated, their lows could be lower than normal and vice versa with their highs.

The expectations cycles exist in every person. There is a hierarchy among expectations. We prioritize what expectations are more important to us than others. Whether it is our career or relationships, we are unable to walk and chew gum at the same time. This hierarchy does change, but the intensity of the feelings that accompany each cycle does not.

3.3 Expectations Rollercoaster

Two siblings are in the same grade and take exactly the same classes at the same school. One of the children is a straight A student and the other is a B student. On report card day, both siblings come home with straight A's. Who will receive the most praise for their report card?

What makes the exact same results appear more positive for one or the other? Simply put, the B student understands how to set expectations better than the A student. The B student has the ability to get A's but chooses not to, instead carefully uses his or her set expectation to stand out when needed. Considering the above scenario, isn't it fair to say that the straight A student is more likely to fail then the B student.

The above example just illustrates an obvious effect of expectations. Although we have not all experienced the same scenario, most of us have felt the double standard effect of expectations.

We typically reward those individuals who exceed expectations, discipline those who miss them, and ignore those who just meet expectations.

Expectations build in a person throughout their lives. These expectations are what drive our successes and failures. We will all meet, exceed and miss expectations throughout our lives. These reactions create new expectations and shape the direction of our lives. Our expectation cycles send us on the rollercoaster of life.

3.4 Our Highs and Lows of Expectations

A rollercoaster ride would be pretty boring if it just stayed level and at slow speeds. What makes a rollercoaster exciting is the heart pounding response they generate in us. It is their ups and especially their downs that get our blood flowing. What would life be if it were level and slow?

Without high expectations there would be no low ones. This Ying and Yang relationship requires that every high be eventually met with a low expectation. This cycle always ends where it starts by setting another expectation. How high these expectations are exceeded will be met by a similar low.

All raised expectations are eventually met with a ceiling, a personal limit, which will result in an eventual failure. When our expectations are being lowered, we will eventually hit a floor, our lower limit, which will eventually lead to a success. We are euphoric at our high and depressed at our low. The expectations cycle is not complete until the high fails and the low holds.

Expectation cycles have time frames. Many expectation cycles can occur at once but not all of them will carry the same weight. Large life expectations, such as careers or relationships, have more impact than smaller ones, such as a bad movie. Every expectations cycle will influence future ones. If we find out that our spouse has cheated on us after 10 years of marriage, our future expectations about marriage will probably not include "till death do us part."

A journey through an expectations cycle will include overlapping similar expectation outcomes. If we are excelling at a sales career and are on the fast track to be promoted to management, we may have one primary expectation that we will be promoted and another to be promoted in two months. We exceed one of these expectations and miss the other. As long as our exceeded expectation outweighs the missed one, our expectations will continue to build. Assume we get promoted to manager. Now as a manager we discover that the job is not as easy as our previous position. Upper management having such high expectations for us is now disappointed, and we start down the expectations cycle. Along the way to the bottom, we may exceed some expectations, but we must go down as much as we had gone up to start the cycle over again. By completing the cycle, we will begin at a new low and start building expectations again. Since upper management will have low expectations for us at this point, we will have more opportunities to exceed their expectations.

When a writer tells a story of their struggles with meeting their low expectations, the success of their writing can start their ascension toward a new high. A great tragedy can lead to triumph of equal magnitude. Great triumph can lead to equal tragedy.

The building of expectations takes longer than the lowering of them. The highest point of expectations is not as noticeable as the lowest point. Time seems to move quickly as expectations are rising. Time slows down while we are in a descending expectations cycle. There will almost always be pain at the bottom of expectations cycles. This characteristic of the expectations cycle is almost entirely attributed to how reluctant and hopeful we are.

3.5 The Birth Right of Expectations

From birth we are bestowed a long list of expectations. Our lives are like a roadmap; influence will determine our path. Our normal attributes will force us to participate in this destiny. At conception our family and community already have placed us on point A on a map and have given us a very small radius in which to travel.

Birth

Within minutes of birth our expectations are already mounted very high. These expectations will result in reactions as we exceed, meet or miss them.

A child who meets and exceeds these expectations more frequently than misses will have a more positive environment. A child who misses more than meets or exceeds these expectations will have a more negative environment.

Expectations set before and at birth are unfair in nature since a person has no control over them. Interesting how the expectations we have the least control over can impact our lives so dramatically. No one chooses to be born.

Gender Expectations

Your gender determines a large part of what is expected of you. If you are born male, expectations are that you will be masculine. If you are born a female, expectations are that you will be feminine.

Masculine characteristics are defined as athletic, strong, competitive, assertive, logical, disciplinarian, and dominant. Feminine characteristics are defined as lack of competitiveness, aggressive nature, independence, passivity, nurturer, and submissiveness. Although we may not agree with the definition of masculine or feminine, society has generally accepted these stereotypes.

In 1974 Jeffery Rubin interviewed a group of 30 mothers and 30 fathers in the first 24 hours after the birth of their children. In the study there were an equal number of boys to girls. Typically in 1974 women were the only parent to hold their newborn child in the first 24 hours after birth. The fathers could observe their child from the hospital nursery window. In the study the fathers were asked a series of questions about their newborn. The interviews with the fathers of the female newborns revealed that most saw their daughter as softer, finer featured, more awkward, more inattentive, weaker, and more delicate. The interview with the fathers of males saw for the most part their sons as firmer, larger featured, better coordinated, more alert, stronger, and hardier. At this age there are no gender-defining feature differences except for genitalia. The only real difference is our expectations of how girls and boys are supposed to be.

These gender expectations that we are born with can significantly influence our lives. Even if our family does not adhere to these expectations, society does; and unless we live on a deserted island, they will influence us in some manner.

Appearance

She has her mother's eyes and her father's nose is a common first impression from family or friends. Since the child is the combination of the parents, the expectation is that the child will look like them. In

49

many cases this is true, but the question is does the baby really have her mother's eyes and her father's nose or is the comment a natural reaction to a common expectation.

Parents have expectations about what their child should look like including height, weight, eye color, and hair color before the child is even born.

Intelligence

Smart parents produce smart children is an immediate expectation put onto a child. If mom went to Harvard, then the expectation is that her child should achieve the same or better.

Expectations in education can dramatically effect a person's life achievements by expecting too much or too little from them.

Religious Expectations

If we are born into a religious family, then likely our faith expectations are already set. Religious families typically expect their children to adopt the same faith and beliefs as at least one of the parents. In some religions, being born male or female creates expectations which can shape their entire life.

Health Expectations

A newborn is immediately expected to be healthy. Health expectations, if missed, can create a dramatic change, as discussed earlier, to the future expectations of the parents.

Inherited Expectations

A large part of what is expected of us comes from our families past. If three generations of males in our family have served in the military, then it is likely if we are the fourth generation to have expectations to serve. This inheritance of expectations can include personality, physical, intelligence, creativity, ingenuity, appearance (as discussed already), and even temperament. If women from a family have a long history of being aggressive, then this expectation will be passed on to future generations of women. These expectations ask the question of whether a person who has inherited them really has these qualities or has been just attempting to live up to them.

3.6 A Life of Expectations

Most people can point to a moment in time where they experienced their biggest failure and their greatest success. Expectations lead us to each of these points at opposite ends of the scale. A person needs to cycle through expectations in order to start the process over. Because we must complete a cycle to start a new one, success is typically credited to failure. Great success can come from great tragedy. Since every extreme high is followed by an extreme low, failure will be attributed to great success. Great tragedy is born out of great triumphs.

The following is a typical life of a normal person growing up in the United States. This decision tree formed by expectations is just to illustrate how these cycles impact a person's life outcomes. Since the life of an average person will encompass thousands of small decisions, we will just focus on the large ones in this example.

Inception

An average American married couple decides to start a family.

This simple statement actually holds large expectations in itself. Typical American communities expect a couple to be married before starting a family. The couple starting the family already has expectations about what type of child they will have and how they will raise this child. Expecting parents typically discuss how their parenting will differ from their peers and their parents. New parents usually set expectations on height, hair color, intellect, appearance, weight, eye color, sex, career, religion, behavior, and even their future grandchildren.

The new parents expect their child will be healthy and larger than normal since one of the parents is extremely tall. Both parents have blue eyes and brown hair, and they expect their child will have the same. The expecting parents are both college-educated intellectuals.

Birth

Thirty-six weeks later their baby is born prematurely. The new parents have a boy with blue eyes and black hair. Since he is born premature, he is only 5 pounds 4 ounces but still healthy. They name him Matthew.

Met or Exceeded Expectations: The baby is born healthy and with blue eyes.

Missed Expectations: The baby is born premature and therefore smaller than normal newborns. He is also born with black hair.

Impact: The hair color expectation is really of no consequence. A premature baby carries a heavy impact on expectations. Although the couple's premature baby is born healthy the term "premature" carries expectations. Studies have shown that parents who have premature births are more likely to have anxiety over their child's health in the beginning. This stress from a social expectation of premature babies will likely lower the parent's expectations of the child's health. The anxiety and stress the parents experience are just signs of their expectations being lowered.

Early Childhood

Both of Matthew's parents did very well in school as children so they expect he will do the same. Since he is born prematurely, they do not expect Matthew to excel at sports because they have lowered his health expectations.

Matthew takes his first steps at 13 months. As an infant he eats well and has very few illnesses. Matthew speaks his first word at 21 months. Matthew learns to ride a bike at age 3.

By the age of 6 he is at least 3 inches taller than his classmates and is the best player on his soccer team. Matthew's first-grade teacher determines he has a learning disability.

Met or Exceeded Expectations: Matthew is athletic, healthy and larger than average.

Missed Expectations: Matthew has not developed academically as his parents expect him to.

Impact: Matthew's parent's anxiety over his health is relieved, and they start to raise expectations about his physical development. Matthew's intellectual expectations come into question. His parents take the anxiety over his health and transfer it to his learning disability. This transference of expectations is a best-case scenario. If Matthew is a sickly child along with the learning disability, the stress and anxiety would be more intense from their expectations being lowered even further for their child's future. From birth to early childhood, Matthew's parents have gone from expecting their child will be a frail intellectual child to an athletic below-average student.

Late Childhood

Matthew's parents were not popular with other children during their late childhoods, so they expect he will be the same. They expect that Matthew will continue to excel at sports. Since Matthew is diagnosed with a learning disability, his parents expect he will struggle in school.

Matthew becomes very popular among his classmates. This popularity follows him through high school. Matthew receives help for his learning disability and manages to bring his grades to above average.

Matthew's student workload is reduced because his parents do not want him to be overwhelmed. The reduced workload left Matthew a lot of free time.

Matthew played soccer in his freshman and sophomore years of high school but chose to quit his junior year to focus more on his social life.

Met or Exceeded Expectations: Matthew is able to conquer his disability and excel in what academics he is exposed to.

Missed Expectations: Matthew gives up on athletics. Matthew is very popular and outgoing.

Impact: Matthew's parents still remain hesitant with his learning disability resulting in not challenging him. Although Matthew meets and exceeds these current expectations, the impact from the original expectation still weighs on his parents. Since they still have lowered expectations and they never really raised his athletic ones because it is not an original expectation, Matthew lacks motivation.

Young Adulthood

Matthew's parents both attended 4-year colleges, but since they have lowered their education expectations, they expect he will attend a community college first. Both Matthew's parents hold jobs in white collar professions, so therefore, they expect that he will work at a desk job.

Matthew enrolls in community college after high school; his first year he focuses on general studies and his ever-growing social life. After seeing his peers focus on their futures, he starts to evaluate his interests. After great thought, he decides he has a real interest in law enforcement. For Matthew's second year of community college he changes his major to Criminal Justice.

He receives his associate's degree in Criminal Justice and immediately enrolls in the police academy. After completing the police academy, he gets a job with his local police department.

Met or Exceeded Expectations: Matthew pursued and completes his secondary education.

Missed Expectations: Matthew chose a career that does not involve a desk.

Impact: Matthew's parent's expectations continue to fall. Although a police officer's career is very respectable, his parents expected he would occupy a desk rather than a police car. Their lowered expectation of Matthew has taken his interest in law enforcement to what his qualifications could permit him to do. Matthew's peers start to influence his education and career expectations.

Beginning Career Adulthood

Matthew's parents reach a bottom of what they expect for his career and intellectual progress. Since Matthew's parents are married and live in the suburbs, they expect Matthew to meet someone and settle down in the town he grew up in.

After 2 years on the police force, Matthew decides his real interest is in the court room as a prosecutor. He decides to leave the police force and go back to school to be an attorney.

Matthew completes his bachelors and law degree at a local state school. While in school, one of his professors convinces him he should move to the city and gain his experience there.

Matthew gets a job in the prosecutor's office in the city. Because Matthew is very interested in law enforcement, he excels quickly in his career at the prosecutor's office. Many long hours and his devoted dedication to his career take its toll on Matthew's love life.

Met or Exceeded Expectations: Matthew exceeds his parent's career and education expectations.

Missed Expectations: Matthew moves to the city and remains single.

Impact: Matthew's parent's expectations begin to rise. Since Matthew's parents value intellectual expectations greatly, they quickly move from reluctant to euphoric. Their lowered expectations on his relationship and residence are clouded by their quickly euphoric feelings towards his success. Matthew's career expectations are influenced by his peers and his leadership.

Early Mid Adulthood

Matthew's parent's expectations increase with every success he has at work. They have visions of him one day being the prosecutor. Their relationship and residence expectations are reduced but again clouded by their inclination towards academics over lifestyle.

Matthew loses more and more of his motivation as he discovers the politics of the prosecutor's office. As Matthew's drive diminishes, his feeling of loneliness starts to take control. Matthew spends less time at the office and more time at social events. Matthew meets Cindy at a local charity event. Immediately, Matthew's focus shifts almost entirely from work to Cindy. After two years of dating they get engaged and married a year later.

Both Matthew and Cindy want children and feel the city is no place for a child. Cindy is also an attorney but feels that having a family is more important than her career at this moment. Conveniently, the prosecutor's position becomes available in his home town, and he and Cindy decide to move to the suburbs and have a family.

Met or Exceeded Expectations: Matthew married Cindy and moves back home to the suburbs.

Missed Expectations: Matthew choses his personal life over his career.

Impact: Matthew's parent's career expectations fall off of a cliff. They are happy he has met Cindy and is moving home to start a family. But they still have a hard time letting go of their visions of him as a prosecutor in the big city. All of these emotions come out in conversations with Matthew as they congratulate him on his marriage but question his decision on leaving the city in the same sentence.

Mid Adulthood

Matthew's parent's influences over him are replaced primarily by Cindy. Although his parents retain a good part of influence over his expectations, Cindy holds the lions share. Cindy expects to start a family with Matthew. Cindy also expects Matthew to support their new family financially. She also expects him to be a good father and be there for them. Matthew's parents expect him to pursue a political career locally.

Matthew settles into his new career as the local prosecutor. He takes what motivation he has left for criminal justice and excels at his new position.

Matthew and Cindy immediately start trying to have a child. Since they are unable to conceive immediately, Cindy starts practicing law locally in the meantime.

Unable to have a baby immediately, Matthew gets reinvigorated on his career outlook. He begins to pursue political avenues in his town by running for town councilman and winning. Matthew starts working long hours, and Cindy picks up more and more local clients.

Soon after Matthew takes his political seat, Cindy gets pregnant. After conception, Cindy refocuses on her family aspirations and leaves her newly started law practice.

Matthew is influenced by Cindy to step down from his political position when the baby is born to ensure he is around for their child.

Matthew and Cindy start to make a list of expectations for their expected child. Matthew and Cindy have a healthy 7 pounds 2 ounce baby girl after 9 months.

Within two years they have another child. This time they have a boy. Matthew is home most nights by 5 p.m., and Cindy settles into her new role as a stay-at-home mother.

Soon Cindy starts to miss her old career as a successful attorney. Matthew grows bored of his career as the town prosecutor. Even though his political career time was short he feels that politics is his true calling.

Matthew resigns his career as the prosecutor and runs for town mayor and wins. Since the Mayoral role is a part-time job, this allows Cindy to go back to work. Matthew becomes the primary caregiver of their children until they leave the house.

Cindy establishes a large successful practice in the area. She continues to support the family until retirement. Matthew continues to be re-elected until he decides to retire with Cindy.

Met or Exceeded Expectations: Matthew is an actively participating father throughout his children's childhood. Matthew pursues and exceeds his parent's political expectations. He starts a family and resided locally.

Missed Expectations: Matthew does not support the family financially.

Impact: Cindy's primary expectation for Matthew is to start a family. Matthew exceeds Cindy's parental expectation. Matthew is able to meet and exceed his parent's primary expectations as well as Cindy's. Matthew and Cindy continue the cycle of expectations with their children.

The above scenario may seem unrealistic to some, but the premise is accurate. Matthew's pursuits in life were born out of expectations. He was able to exceed expectations as soon as they were lowered by those who influenced them. He missed expectations as soon as they had peaked. His life was lived within the expectations that had been set for him.

The expectations influence on our pursuits in life lead us from one success to failure to another success. From birth, our map is already drawn; whether we end up on the east side or the west is of no matter, we still will remain on the map. Our need to stay on this life map is controlled by our normal attributes. As we will see in the following, "Normal" human beings are followers of abnormal people.

The Art of Expectations

4

Why Groups Do
What they Do

Throughout history man has accomplished magnificent feats. Man has also been the cause of great atrocities. As people we are unable to build a pyramid, but as members of groups we have built many. Pyramids around the world were constructed by strong leaders with their powerful influence. The power of these leaders was so strong that their followers enslaved generations of their fellow man to build these abnormal structures. Most great group actions are at the expense of others.

As we discussed earlier, groups perform abnormal actions. A person as a member of a group will dismiss their normal limits and will go beyond their typical threshold. This phenomenon makes the actions of groups more extreme than an individual person. Alone, we may be able to walk 5 miles, but as part of a group we could march 50 or until we cannot walk anymore. A group's actions will almost always go to extremes. A person who is a member of a group will let go of their attributes of normal and mindlessly follow their leader's abnormal requests.

A member's actions do not reflect their personal nature but more that of their leaders. Since members of groups are "hypnotized," their actions should not be held against them. The leader carries the fault of the group's actions.

Groups do what they do, because their leaders tell them to. As a member of a group, our actions are controlled by the leader who influences us.

4.1 The Decisions Groups Make

Since groups do what their leaders tell them to do, it is natural that their decisions are determined by their leaders. To truly understand the decisions a group makes, we must understand the rise and fall of a leader's power. A leader of the moment's power, as described earlier, is typically very short lived, and they are motivated by a larger group. A military officer who leads his platoon into a battle is driven by the leader who influenced him to fight that battle.

We will examine the cycle of the rare self-motivated leader since their power commands the most abnormal actions.

Rare leaders, as previously discussed, are abnormal people. An abnormal person still experiences expectations cycles, but their highs are higher and their lows are lower than a normal person. These higher highs and lower lows impress normal people to follow their expectations cycles. Since their limits are abnormal, their followers will follow them beyond their own personal limits. A primary attribute of a rare leader is their complete lack of foresight. Without foresight it is impossible for them to see how their actions are limited.

The leader's passion and commitment to their cause hypnotizes their current members and attracts new ones. These rare leaders are able to command their members to carry out their personal expectations.

In the beginning these leaders test the waters of the limits of what their group is capable of. With every successful action, they will ask more of their group members. The higher this leader goes in their expectations the more members they are able to attract. In the beginning this leader will have a clear purpose and defined agenda.

As the power of this rare leader peaks, so do the extreme actions of the group. As group membership grows too large, the message of the leader becomes spread thin. The leader's decisions become erratic, and his power over the group starts to teeter. The leader's actions and therefore the actions of the group become less purposeful and clear. Their power has peaked, and the group will start to disband slowly. At this point in a leader's cycle they will attempt dramatic action.

For example, this is the point where Jim Jones led over 900 people to mass suicide. Jim Jones started becoming paranoid and delusional when some members started questioning his cause. This led him to test his influence over his followers. He tested the loyalty of his followers on multiple occasions with mock mass suicide before the actual day.

When Congressman Ryan visited Jones Town and some members requested to leave with him, Jim Jones and several members of his group killed the Congressman and other innocent bystanders. He then used his last bit of influence over his group to lead them to a mass suicide. Jim Jones commanded so much influence of his followers that 276 of the over 900 dead were children. Parents took the lives of their own children for this rare abnormal leader.

Time takes the power of these leaders away. Time erodes the power of these leaders. The decisions of a leader during his loss of power are hopeful. The rare and once powerful leader will yearn for their previous influence. Their message has less impact, and their followers will start to regain self-control over their actions.

What makes these leaders so powerful is their ability to become martyrs. History books will tell their stories and spread their influences for generations to come. Some leaders will have statues, roads, cities, schools (among other structures) named after them. A leader may be thought of as negative in their time but martyred in the future.

If a leader is killed or dies at the peak of his power, he becomes a legend. A leader is most powerful when he dies at his peak of power.

Groups have time limits. Normal is the baseline for who we are. Group members will always return back to normal, unless their leader dies at their peak, since group membership has a time limit.

4.2 What are Group Expectations

In the thick of battle a soldier's expectations are to live. The strategic results of the battle are of no consequence to the soldier. A soldier does not win a battle on his or her own. They fight to survive the ordeal while pushing forward at the command of their leader. A soldier is merely a weapon of their leader, and the battle is just a stepping stone on the rise or fall of their leader's expectations.

Membership in groups only impacts the attribute which attracted us in the first place. If a person joins a group because of their admiration for the leader's abnormal hopefulness, the remaining "Normal" attributes are intact.

The soldier, described above, is a pawn of their leader's agenda. The soldier may have joined the fight in admiration of a leader with an abnormal belief in the fairytale of freedom. They will still pursue happiness and exhibit all other normal attributes, but their now influenced belief in fairytales will push them to take abnormal actions in the name of the leader.

Many soldiers return from war with nightmares of the actions they had committed. These soldiers live with the consequences of their leader's actions. As discussed before, group membership is just a matter of time. The missed or exceeded expectations of a soldier's leadership will impact their future expectations. This trauma caused by the actions they committed under the influence of their leader is not the result of indecision. A person who has taken the life of another must live with the consequences of their actions. They have taken someone elses mother's, father's, brother's, sister's, or friend's life. If they committed this act under the influence of a leader, then the reason for killing them is unclear. Since groups act out the expectations of their leaders, members will not be able to explain why they did what they did. The soldier will live with the pain of their leader's actions. Members carry the burden of their leaders. The soldier will continue to cycle from high to low expectations, but their previous actions will affect how high and low they are capable of achieving. They might find that their highs are not as high as they were before, and their lows are lower.

As a member of a group, we only expect to live, die, eat, and breathe. Leaders have expectations; members act out their expectations cycle while attempting to stay alive or die with the approval of their leader.

One man cannot conquer the world, but one man who controls many can.

When we act on our own expectations, our actions are limited to normal limits. Groups break all barriers of normal since it takes an abnormal person to lead them.

The primary difference between an individual person's expectations and a group's are their limits. A normal person's belief in fairytales could cause them to confront a bully in search of personal peace. A group in the search of peace may confront a nation. Normal people will only go so far, while members of a group will go as far as their leader expects. Peace is the result of war.

4.3 Limits of Group Expectations

Groups may show no limits to what actions they are capable of committing, but the laws of nature do have limits. Limits are set by nature and not by man. If we construct a building that has several stories, we must have the appropriate amount of support so it does not collapse. Support is needed to prevent a structure from collapsing on its own weight. Support required because of gravity which cannot be changed by man. The limits of structures are not up to us but the natural forces in which we live.

Expectations have natural supports. An individual person acting on their own never tests these supports, but groups commonly bounce off of them.

In The Great Depression, the limit of greed was met by an equal limit of poverty. When group members are pushed towards these natural limits, they cannot imagine a world any different. The Great Depression shows us that if we hit one natural limit we will hit the opposite limit.

Imagine bouncing a ball in a small room with enough force to hit the ceiling. Naturally, the ball will hit the ground after bouncing off the ceiling, but more than likely it will not have enough force to complete the cycle again and eventually settle on the ground. Groups exert the force, and nature confines their actions. What goes up must go down, and in expectations the down typically matches the up.

After an extreme event caused by a powerful group, the impacts are felt in some cases for generations. The Great Depression impacted a

70

generation on taking risk. It was not until the early 1980s that the Dow Jones Industrial Average exploded from its otherwise slow and steady growth. This steady slow movement is the effect of the ball, abnormal action, settling after such a strong force was applied to it. Eventually, when the effects of the abnormal event are forgotten, a new group will form and attempt to "bounce the ball" of risk again resulting in history repeating itself.

Most natural limits are obvious. The truth behind the saying "hindsight is twenty-twenty" reflects this. Members of a group that approach these natural limits are aware of them but under the spell of the group, choose to ignore them. History remembers these people under this spell as delusional.

Money has some obvious natural limits. If a nation has a $1 trillion credit limit and they have $999 billion of outstanding credit, if they borrowed one more dollar they would be at their natural limit. Members of groups driven by greed may understand these limits but refuses to believe them. They will continue to invest in the face of this obvious natural limit. The larger and stronger the group, the bigger the impact they can have. History is filled with events like these even though the natural limits have always existed. A dollar borrowed is a dollar borrowed; beware of creative financing. Interest rates can only go to zero before prices must come down to meet demand; this is a common cause of deflation.

Natural limits can change with the discovery of new innovations. Unfortunately, these changes are gradual, and groups outpace the expansion of limits through innovation. For example the masterminds behind the building of pyramids may have wanted to construct a thousand-foot high pyramid, but the knowledge of construction had not evolved to that point. But without the construction of these pyramids, a thousand-foot building may not be possible today. Pushing the natural limits can also lead to the expansion of the limits they are testing. Great success is always credited to great failure.

Groups are the only entities capable of meeting these natural limits. As long as there has been currency and credit, groups have pushed their limits. The ocean has a floor, and we cannot breathe in space. These are our natural limits as human beings.

4.4 Group Leaders with Abnormal Expectations

Normal people have difficulty imagining the world of tomorrow since it involves letting go of today. Those who can let go of today are visionaries and prophets. Great leaders who have taken civilization into the future share this ability. These visionaries and prophets have abnormal beliefs in fairytales. These great leaders have expectations that exceed a normal person since they have this abnormal attribute.

A person with an abnormal attribute will have abnormal expectations. Visionaries expect the world to change beyond the normal imaginable outcome. These abnormal expectations of visionaries and prophets have formed groups that have turned villages into cities.

As Gustave Le Bon pointed out in his book "The Crowd," civilization was created by a small group of individuals who commanded the will of the crowd. He also stated that without powerful groups civilization would likely have crumbled. Society has not always chosen the most rational direction, but they do choose what their leader wants.

Our personal expectations are within reach. We have the ability to achieve our personal expectations because they have been accomplished by someone else before. An abnormal person who leads a group expects the unexpected. This person may expect to land on mars, but our natural limits may land us on the moon.

When these abnormal expectations are achieved by the group leader, they will, like a "Normal"

73

person, raise their expectations again. Although a person may have one abnormal attribute, their other instincts (attributes) remain intact. They will continue to raise these expectations until they eventually supersede the natural limits of the time. Their power grows with expectations.

4.5 Artificial Groups

During a holiday season, it's not uncommon for a person to pay more for a product than the manufacturers suggested retail price. Our anxiety prevents us from waiting for supply to catch up with demand and causes us to overpay. This anxiety, which causes similar symptoms of addiction, typically is not of our own doing but engineered by another for profit.

The 1928 Edward Bernays book "Propaganda" changed marketing tactics forever. Edward Bernays was Sigmund Freud's nephew. Edward Bernays discussed ways to market products and political will through propaganda. Instead of politicians and or companies forcing products or political views on the public, they must establish a need first then provide their product or view as a solution.

"Start the fire then sell the extinguisher."

Edward Bernays called this process "engineering consent." His research and development of engineering consent earned him the nickname "The Father of Spin."

Businesses and politicians regularly employ the use of propaganda to further their success. Propaganda uses our normal attributes against us as an animal trainer uses their methods to command obedience.

Over recent holiday seasons, consumers have regularly paid more than 50 percent over the retail price for popular video gaming systems of that season. The overpaying for a mass-produced item prior to the holiday is caused by companies creating a short supply of their product (or slow distribution), a child's perceived immediate need caused by propaganda, and limited time. Most of these game systems are available at their suggested retail price several days after the holiday. The influence and the timeline created this artificial group frenzy, and when one of these elements disappears, so does the event. Think about how powerful these artificial groups have become when they regularly command their members to camp out for days to buy a mere electronic device. The above examples are referring to members of Artificial Groups.

A person who has succumbed to propaganda and unknowingly joins these Artificial Groups will have no problem paying twice the suggested retail price of a product. A person who has not will view the other person as out of their mind.

When a group is formed by these artificial tactics, the power of the group's leadership is very limited in time. Artificial groups are erratic due to their engineered nature. The leadership's motivations are unnatural, and the group's actions will reflect the same. The unpredictable actions of these groups make them dangerous. Artificial groups will typically make more attempts at our natural limits and in some cases push beyond them with dire consequences. Imagine a government that was able to convince its citizens that a nuclear attack is only solvable by the same response which would result in the end of the world.

4.6 Politics, Economics and Community Expectations

We are born with the expectation to live up to our family's image. Unfortunately, this is not enough to be normal. Society has another set of expectations for us. Politically in the United States we are Republicans, Democrats or Independents. We are expected to participate in our local education system, which could include home schooling if it is common in our community. We are expected to obey the laws. We have expectations to work and contribute to the local economy. These are just some of the expectations we are born with even though many of these are looking many years into our futures. We are expected to be a normal member of the community. If we move, the new community sets expectations for us.

Although the surrounding community and the country we live in have expectations for us, we have expectations for them. We expect the community that we live in to provide a safe environment. We expect the country we live in to protect us from the outside world. We expect that the food we buy is safe. We expect the government to protect us from financial fraud. Unfortunately, we expect too much from them, and vice versa they expect too much from us. We see these over expectations in the communities, economics and politics we live in. One day we are capitalist, and the next day we are socialist. We expect financial windfalls to continue forever. When the going gets tough we expect it will not get worse. This roller coaster of political, economic and community change is driven by our unrealistic expectations of the world we live in.

Many of these unrealistic expectations are set by groups. Groups raise and lower the bar well above and below our natural limits as discussed earlier. Many politicians and corporations take advantage of these unrealistic expectations and form artificial groups to exploit them. They use the already abnormal environment to "engineer consent" for their political or product support.

Politics in the United States commonly changes from one political party to the other by capitalizing on missed political expectations. Americans expected that home prices would continue to go up and credit would continue to be loose. As soon as the real estate market sank, the majority of citizens elected the opposite political party in hopes for a solution. It is safe to say that in the near future America will flip flop again. Unfortunately, the solution to most problems is typically the hardest one.

Hybrid cars have slowly taken over the roads by using images of nature to appeal to the ever growing environmental groups in United States, even though the fuel efficiency of these cars do not amount to a savings over a similar size vehicle because of their hefty price tags. Most automobile manufacturers in the near future intend to release electric cars. Since a majority of the electricity in America is produced by burning coal, these vehicles will produce a larger carbon footprint than a similar sized vehicle since they need to be plugged in. These automobile manufacturers aren't advertising how this will affect your electric bill or the damage on the environment; instead they are advertising the huge savings at the pump. Profits drive companies not the environment. When Americans want big cars again, they will be glad to make them.

The communities we live in touch our lives more than any other influence. We trust our valuables to the local police and our children to the local schools. Just because we live in a town or a city does not mean that the entire area is our community. Our community is the environment that we live in, the streets we walk on, the neighbors we talk to, and the shops we patronize.

We are members of the communities we live in whether we like it or not. This membership has a group's influence. Our communities can influence us to commit abnormal acts. If our community is involved in a natural disaster, that event can have us take abnormal risks to save fellow neighbors. When on vacation if we meet another person from our community, even if we have never met or seen them before, we instantly relate to them.

The Art of Expectations

5

Determining Outcomes
Through Expectations

At this point we understand that our similarities outweigh our differences. These similarities are what make our actions predictable. We understand that our attributes of normal compel us to join groups and press the natural limits. We understand that the higher we go, the further we will fall. Children continue to feel they are better than their parents and the generations before them. History repeats itself because it is normal for us to want to be so different from others. The unfortunate side effect of feeling special blinds us to how similar we really are. The tools and the entertainment may have changed, but we are still the same as we have been for thousands of years with respect to our normal attributes.

Only one difference exists from yesterday, and that is that we live longer. We stretch out our action over time since our lifecycle has become longer. Our actions stay the same; a generation to forget just takes longer.

Our actions as normal individuals are pushed to extremes by group influence. Although our actions are more excessive as a member of a group, they are still predictable. Whether we walk five miles as an individual or are influenced to march 50 miles as a member of a group, we are still walking. The question is how far we will go under the influence of a group. The answer to this question is twofold. First, it depends on how powerful and large the group has become. Second is the natural limit of the action. If we physically cannot walk more than 47.5 miles without collapsing no matter what influence is over us, this is our natural limit. We will not exceed our leader's expectations until we approach the 47.5-mile mark whereby we will collapse on our natural limit.

By measuring natural limits we can predict, with a high degree of accuracy, outcomes of group actions in politics, economics and communities. We will also be able to predict and change outcomes of our personal actions.

To predict an outcome we must first find an action. This can be a personal or group action. When we look at our personal actions, we need to realize that we can only change these outcomes by being aware of where our current path will lead us. When we are looking at a group's action, we must first separate ourselves from this group so that we are not influenced by them. The natural limit of a group's action cannot be changed. When attempting to determine the outcome of a group's action, we must focus on determining their true natural limits.

Second, we need to measure the expectations. As discussed above when we measure our own actions we have control over them so, therefore, it is difficult to calculate them. How we measure our or a group's expectations must be a finite calculation not open to interpretation. This involves finding out where in the expectations cycle we or the groups are by applying a number to it. There must be a defined limit in order to proceed with determining an actions outcome.

Third, we need to determine its natural limit. This step involves history and a general understanding of the world we live in. If a road only goes for 10 miles, then it is not possible to continue down this road for 20 miles. If we earn $1,000 a week, then our payments cannot exceed this. When we die, we are unable to continue to live. These are our natural limits.

These three steps will be evaluated and explained in the following section. By understanding how to use this information to determine outcomes, it can provide clarity and profitability to our life.

5.1 A Simple Existence

If we are all involved in a community, the economy and or a political group as already discussed, how can we identify what group actions with which we are associated with?

Just as the age-old question asks, "What came first the chicken or the egg," the same can be asked, "What came first the leader or the group." It is commonly accepted that the egg came first because the egg came from an animal that evolved into a chicken. The same can be said about what came first with a group or a leader. Groups create leaders. It takes the influence of a group to create a leader. Where the egg or the group originated from is still a mystery with theoretical answers. More likely the first group is our membership to our species as humans.

Since our normal attributes are instincts, it is fair to say that when we first evolved as humans we had them. In order to measure expectations and, therefore, predict outcomes, we must understand who we really are. We are animals that live longer than most other animals in the world and, therefore, have longer, harder lives to identify cycles. When we look at a colony of ants, we see that their actions are very deliberate and with purpose. Each action of an individual ant contributes to the colony. Size and life expectancy make ants' actions more predictable because their limits are easier to define. If we look at these ants under a microscope, their actions look erratic and unorganized; although, when we step back they appear uniform and organized. Although ants seem to look the same as others in the colony, the closer we look, the more we see slight differences from one to the other. We are those ants in our actions, and we must be able to step back to see our purpose and direction and identify our natural limits. We must step back from a group and ignore the erratic behavior and determine the real possible outcome. This requires us to separate ourselves from the situation, which is easier said than done.

First, we will discuss simplifying group actions. Step one in achieving this quest for the truth requires us to remove the complexities from the actions and situations around us. If we understand that the little things don't matter and it is the larger actions that matter, this will simplify spotting the real action. Unfortunately, we live in a society that praises those who sound intelligent and over complicate simple problems and solutions. When we go to war, politicians cite a growing concern or complex environment, which leaves us no other choice. Typically, war is the result of one person fighting another because of a difference of opinion. To truly take a step back from a situation we must understand in simple terms what really is happening. If a first grader cannot understand it, than we are still under its influence, and we must take another step back. We need to take the grey out of situations and actions. There are only yes or no answers, not maybe. And it is either two or three, not several; clarity is required. Nothing must be open to interpretation.

The second step requires us to dismiss those people who make declarative statements about the actions that we are studying. For example, when a financial group moves towards high expectations, these people will declare that the financial windfall will never end. This step is extremely important because in the face of a strong group influence these people will make us question our measurements. We must trust our independent view over someone who is neck deep in the influence of the group. These people are attempting to be the momentary leaders, as discussed earlier. They are almost as delusional as the primary leader of the group. We see these people as visionaries if we are under the influence of the group. When we feel admiration towards another person and look to emulate them, more than likely we are under the influence of a group.

Lastly, we must maintain our distance from the group and its actions. We cannot let the influence of this group cloud our simple outlook. Under the influence of a group, we will give explanations for the unexplainable. Typically, these groups are looking for a future event to justify their means. Most abnormal actions and situations that involve groups are obvious, as discussed earlier, "hind sight is twenty-twenty."

Stepping back from our own personal lives involves more self-control. Since the influence over us usually involves family, friends, peers, or management, these situations and our actions are difficult to evaluate. Being able to take a step back from our lives and make a simple logical evaluation of our actions will create fewer regrettable moments.

The first step in removing ourselves from our actions long enough to really take a good measurement of our expectations involves simplifying them. We must first understand what our expectations are and take a simpler evaluation of where we are. If we expect to become the CEO of the company we have been working for over the past five years, we need to look at this from a simple view and match our effort with our goals. If we just "punch in and punch out" every day, dread Mondays, and start dreaming of Friday, Monday afternoon, then this expectation is simply unrealistic. We must take a cold hard look at who we are and what we are doing in comparison to our expectations. Honesty is the best policy especially when we evaluate our own expectations. We should write down our expectations and determine what we can do to meet them. If it is beyond our natural limits, then our expectations need to be reevaluated. We are our own worst enemies, dare to try and don't fear to fail. Our own natural limits should not be what we think we are capable of but rather what we are humanly capable of. Research, not personal feelings, are how we determine our natural limits.

Next, we need to beware of those individuals who attempt to alter our expectations. "One rotten egg spoils the bunch" – don't be a part of the bunch. When our expectations are building, we need to look out for those people who try to make us overshoot our expectations. Equally we need to look out for those people who want to "rain on our parade." Remember that misery loves company. These individuals whole desire in life is to cloud our judgment. Keep things simple; the second they become complex we have been infected by one of these distractions.

Lastly, as with groups we must remain objective. We must continue to be honest with ourselves. Are we trying hard enough? Is the situation really that dire? We should make a simple and logical evaluation of our expectations. The way to evaluate these expectations is alone without friends, family, peers, management, television, internet, or any type of communication. Distractions add complexities to the normally simple actions and situations. We must not be influenced by any outside source while taking a step back and reviewing our expectations.

Today our influence and attention is viewed as a commodity. Someone is always biding for it. The groups that attempt to take possession of our influence result in more and more distractions every day. Being able to separate ourselves from these distractions will reveal a world that makes more sense than the one we are currently aware of. When historic events are occurring, this ability allows us to benefit from or avoid the results of the outcome.

"Challenge every piece of bad news and look for the good and equally view all good news as potentially bad."

5.2 Identifying Predictable Expectations

We have simplified and understood what is going on around us, now we must identify expectations we can measure and predict. Unfortunately, not all expectations are predicable. I may expect to live to 80 years old, but no matter how well I take care of myself, disease or an accident can change this. Expectations that are predictable are measurable with the least amount of outside influence. A hospital may expect that Medicare will continue to cover certain patients in the future, but politicians can alter this expectation without notice. Measuring all possible outcomes and aligning these expectations makes the odds of a certain outcome too high. Too many variables create diluted results. The answer again must be specific and not open to interpretation. The outcome to an action must have a yes or no, up or down, or left or right solution. If a car is driving towards a brick wall and the driver does not hit their brake, they will hit the wall.

The stock market is a perfect example of a yes or no result. It is either going up or down. The market is either bullish or bearish. Yes or no is the only outcome on whether to buy or sell stocks. For the market to go up, it requires more investors to buy rather than sell stocks – yes or no to stocks and no maybes. This makes the stock markets measurable. When we are measuring the stock market's expectations, we are not looking fundamentally or technically at individual stocks, instead we measure their expectations. A fundamentally strong stock has a hard time going up in a bear market just as a fundamentally weak stock has a hard time going down in a bull market. This is because the analysts and underlying companies who are setting these expectations are influenced by either a bullish sentiment or bearish one. If a market has high expectations, analysts will more likely have loftier goals for weak companies. This is apparent in a bull market when the most volatile stocks outperform the more fundamentally sound ones. When a market has high expectations, the group will push the natural limits of risk. Higher risk equals higher reward. With bearish expectations analysts will sink further and faster than reality and set the stage for another bull market since their expectations are falling faster than profits.

Another good example of a measurable expectation exists in politics. If we ask 100 different people – who are classified as independents and who are not influenced greatly by either party – a yes or no question whether they believe a politician is doing a good job, their answer would paint a good picture of what expectations are for this person. If 55 percent believe that he or she is doing a good job, than it is fair to say they have high expectations for the politician. Just because these independents have high expectations for this politician does not mean that they are destined to fail. It just means that these independents already expect good things from this politician, and they will be harder to please. There is a point where a politician will meet his natural limits, and it becomes humanly impossible for him to exceed them. This is the point where this politician has no other direction to go but down since these independents have reached their natural high limit of expectations. To determine this natural limit of a politician we need to study the historic highs and lows in this political arena. Research determines natural limits, not our opinions.

In our personal lives we either get a promotion or not. In relationships we can't predict whether we will live happily ever after. A relationship could end in divorce, widowed or staying together. In this case we are angry, sad or happy. Three outcomes make this type of personal expectation too difficult to predict. We may be able to predict emotional responses to other missed expectations that could lead to divorce. If I interview for an internal job position and they are making the decision on Friday, I either will get it or not. The primary differences between predictable personal outcomes are the possible results. They must be yes or no, only two outcomes with no other foreseeable variables. There will be random things in life that are unpredictable. It is possible a thousand foot tsunami, caused by an asteroid hitting the Atlantic, could wipe most of the east coast of the United States off the map. This type of disaster or wild card cannot be included as a possible outcome since it is highly unlikely. If an action's outcome has less than a 1 percent chance, then it is fair to not include it as a possible outcome. As mentioned before if we continue to take risks where one of the possible outcomes is zero, then eventually we will end up with zero. We will either love or hate. It may start as like, but our expectations will make it love and then turn to hate. Personal expectation outcomes are purely emotional. Our emotions give us the motivations to push or pull back as a result of exceeding or missing expectations.

5.3 Interpreting Expectations Environment

Most of our lives revolve around large-scale group expectations. Whether we are being affected by the rise or fall of expectations, they influence our perception of the environment around us. If our local and or regional economy is expanding on high expectations of growth of a specific product or service, then we will perceive and expect the world around us is getting financially better. If our expectations are falling, then we will assume they are getting worse. A positive response is always met with an equally negative one. Predictable outcomes are the ones that have either a positive or negative effect on our perception of the world around us.

Most of our good feelings are compounded positive events around us that act as a domino effect on building our enthusiasm. But as with dominos eventually they will all fall, and we will need to reset them. We will have some negative events in this otherwise positive environment. The multiple events that contribute to the larger event are predictable, but if the overall expectations are building, the positives will outweigh the negatives.

In a bull market, more stocks are going up than going down. Some individual market sectors can move higher than others in a bull market. If the overall stock market is building expectations, it would be safer to buy stocks that have low expectations, since they are more likely to beat expectations than a company whose expectations have outpaced the market.

When our expectations are falling, negative events outweigh positive ones. Our perception of the world around us is clouded by overwhelming negative feelings. Although there will be some positive events, the negative ones will outweigh the positive ones.

If we are in a bear market, more stocks are going down than up. When a market is lowering expectations, it is better to sell stocks that have high expectations since they will more likely miss expectations than a company that has outpaced the descent of the market as a whole.

On any given day or moment in time, it is safe to say that there are equally good and bad pieces of news. When we read a newspaper, there are both positive and negative articles. A positive article for one person may be a negative one for another. The saying "there are two sides to every story" exemplifies this fact. If country A goes to war with country B and country A wins, then country A will view this as positive while country B will view this as a negative. Depending on where we are in an expectations cycle will determine how we view news events. If we are building expectations, then we will see the negative over the positive. If we have met our expectations limit and are descending, then we will view news events as more positive than negative. If we read a headline where four people were involved in a car accident and two of them died, if we are lowering expectations most likely we will view the two survivors as positive over the negative of the two deaths. If we were building expectations, then we likely will view the two deaths as more negative over the positive of the two survivors. These types of positive or negative reactions give us insight as to

93

whether a group is building or lowering expectations. The way a person or group of people reacts to news is the most obvious way to determine what part of the expectations cycle they are in. A hopeful response is a sign of lowering expectations while a reluctant one is a sign of building expectations.

The environment around us creates a backdrop to events that enfold in it. When expectations are building, there will be more positive events then negative. When expectations are being lowered, there will be more negative events then positive. The direction of expectations determines the backdrop. To determine the change in direction of expectations, we must be able to measure them. As discussed earlier, we must challenge every piece of bad news and view it as good and vice versa.

5.4 Measuring Expectations

We must be able to measure a group or our own expectations in order to predict the outcomes. We are only dealing with two possible outcomes, so we are either building expectations or lowering them. After we identify an action, we would like to predict with only two possible outcomes; we need to apply a numerical value and natural limit to it.

When we measure expectations of groups, we do not focus on a single member's intensity but rather the sum of the whole group. If we are measuring the expectations of a group of people, we do not focus on an individual person's intensity level of expectations; instead, we value high expectations as one and negative expectations as a minus one. Just because one person may be more passionate than another, positive is one and negative is minus one. Neutral expectations are impossible in a human. If a person has no expectations then they are not a part of the action and therefore should not be evaluated in the first place. Remember, in order to evaluate expectations, we can only look at those who are a part of the action. Why would we ask a British citizen if they have high or low expectations of a United States politician in a political race? Their expectations play no role in the future outcome of who is elected because they are not able to vote.

Assume we would like to predict a future re-election of a United States politician applying this concept with only two candidates. Using this method of prediction outcomes, we would focus on the daily or weekly approval ratings of the candidate running. We would only focus on the expectations of people who are able to vote for this politician. If the election is for the Governor of New Jersey, a Virginia resident should not be evaluated. In the United States most, if not all, regional and national media outlets perform weekly or daily approval ratings. Also, there are institutions that just poll Americans daily to determine sentiment. We would first find media outlets and or institutions that poll potential voters on approval and choose polls with the least amount of overlap and cover the majority of voters. If this election covers an entire state or larger, we must ensure the polls cover most if not all regions. If the election is on a smaller scale such as a small town, then we could look for polls of different age groups, affiliations, or regions of the town. Again, our goal is to cover the most voters with the least amount of overlap. Then we would evaluate the best time frame for us to use. If the media or institutions mostly conduct daily polls, then we should evaluate daily expectations. If equally they conduct daily and weekly polls, then we should just look at weekly numbers. Keep in mind that it is important that we use the most unbiased polls available. Understanding that most media outlets in the United States have some sort of political bias, we should avoid polls from political-party-driven media sources such as purely Democrat, Republican or other political party news agencies. Now we would gather and evaluate the data. Regardless of whether we are evaluating daily or weekly polls, we would set a value to either positive or negative approval ratings. If more people in a poll approve than disapprove of the candidate, then that specific poll on that date is assigned a value of one. If more people disapprove than approve of the candidate, then we would assign that poll, on that date, a minus one. Since most of these institutions give these voters a way out of committing to approval or disapproval, there is a chance that they will have equal ratings so in this case we would assign this poll a zero. Although this value of zero contradicts the idea of only two outcomes, the chance of this poll being neutral for every time period evaluated is extremely rare. We use the value of zero so that it does not contribute or take away from the period measurement. After gathering the scores, we would tally them for that time period. The following is an example of what measurements could look like:

Poll 1: (name of institution here) If this poll had 48 percent approve and 44 percent disapprove, then it would be assigned a scored: 1

Poll 2: If this poll had 41 percent approve and 44 percent disapprove, it would be scored: -1

Poll 3: If this poll had 44 percent approve and 44 percent disapprove, it would be assigned a score of: 0

Poll 4: 1
Poll 5: 1
Poll 6: 0
Poll 7: -1
Poll 8: 0
Poll 9: 1
Poll 10: 1

Total: 3

In the above example the candidate's expectations have a value of three. This number means that overall the voters are more positive than negative on the candidate. Therefore, voters have higher than lower expectations for him or her. This means in this measured period that voters expect more from this candidate.

The above scenario just gives us a snapshot of voter opinion and does not allow us to predict the future outcome of this election. If this poll was conducted the day before or on the day of the election, we might assume that he or she would win. As discussed earlier we understand the direction of expectations determines the direction of their momentum. To determine direction of expectations we must find the natural limit of the expectation. In the above example, the candidate expectations are valued at three. The best way to determine this candidate's natural limit is to continue to evaluate the daily or weekly poll data and study the effects of the expectations values from period to period. If this candidate has a one value on the next period, then we could start to consider the three as a possible limit. The only way to truly determine this limit is by observing and recording a complete expectations cycle. If the numbers over the next periods are: 1, 2, -1, 0, -2, -3, -1, 1, 3, 1, 0, etc. then we could begin to validate that the expectations at a positive three could be the upper limit of this candidate's natural high limit. As discussed earlier if we touch the limit of high expectations, we will touch the lower limit of minus three. If this candidate has a three value now, then we could assume that if the election was four periods away they would lose the election. Vice versa, if this candidate had touched a minus three in poll expectations and the election was again four periods away, then we could assume they would win the election.

By taking these measurements, we are applying a value to a group's expectations over time. By understanding the amount of pressure that weighs on a possible outcome, we can surmise a probable conclusion.

Measuring our own expectations is more difficult than of a group because of our own involvement. Instead of looking at separate group polls, we are polling our own expectations. If we were attempting to predict whether we will get a promotion at work, we would start by determining who or what will determine whether we get promoted. After we research what action will determine our promotion, we would need to start measuring them. Let's assume we determined that our promotion depends on the following: our direct manager's support, their manager's support, our daily sales, tardiness, organization, good communication skills, company dedication, and leadership skills. We would organize these eight expectations and give a plus one for exceeding, a minus one for missing, and a zero for meeting them daily. Our tally for each day may look something like the following:

Example Day:

Manager Approval: Our manager is happy with our overall performance from the day before so we would value this expectation at: 1

Manager's Manager: Our Manager's Manager is pleased since our previous week sales exceeded their weekly expectations earning us an expectations value of: 1

Daily Sales: We missed our daily sales expectations so we earned a value of: -1

Tardiness: We were on time so we neither exceeded or missed expectations; therefore, we apply an expectation value of: 0

Organization: Our desk was left unorganized the day before, and our manager noticed so this expectation value is: -1

Good Communication Skills: We neither missed or exceeded this expectation, thereby, applying an expectations value of: 0

Dedication: Since we left on time even though our sales were poor, we would assign an expectations value of: -1

Leadership Skills: Because we ignored a teammate who needed our help with a customer on our way to lunch, we would record a value of: -1

Total: -2

In the above example our personal expectations for getting this promotion were lowered. Notice how each day, week, hour, and minute affects the other expectations. From the above evaluation we would likely not be promoted if the decision was being made that day, but if we have 10 days until the decision is made this may be the springboard to get us promoted. Since most of these expectations are under our direct control, we could use this to help ensure we are on the right expectations slope as we approach the decision day. As in the group expectations measurement, we must determine our limits. In the above scenario obviously a plus eight or a minus eight would be the best or worst we could achieve. Since most of these expectations are tied to another in some way, reaching these extreme values would be highly unlikely. If in the next days leading up to the decision, we recorded the following values: -3, -1, 0, 2, 1, 3, 2, -1, -3. We could assume that if there were five days left to the decision we made our probability of getting promoted greater. This is because we are at a low point in expectations and exceeding would be easier than failing. If we were at three, then our chance of failure would be greater than success since our expectations are already at their limit.

In the stock market, equities do not trade on fundamentals alone; otherwise, they would only trade several times a year. Instead, stocks trade on what the market expects of them and whether they exceed or miss their expectations. To accentuate this fact, we will discuss a simple stock market expectations indicator that was developed using this theory, which provides an accurate measurement of Wall Street's and companies' earnings expectations.

Taking measurements in expectations for our personal as well as observed group actions gives us the likely outcome.

5.5 Predictable Outcomes with Expectations Today and Yesterday

Looking back to just yesterday reveals many outcomes that should have been predictable. Yesterday is always full of events that we should have seen coming.

These predictable outcomes in the past can include a simple expectation of a movie we saw in the theatre. If we are disappointed in the movie we just saw because it missed our expectations that were built up by a trailer, our outcome could have been predicted if we researched who produced or wrote the film. Screenwriters typically have a style as well as directors. If we did not like their work in the past, it is likely we will not like it in the future.

On September 11, 2001, a terrorist group attacked the United States. This event immediately changed our expectations of safety in the United States. Although we knew terrorists existed and they had killed thousands around the world, we failed to recognize the threat because our expectations of safety had risen to their limit. Before this event we did not recognize the risks we were taking. Before this attack we never viewed an airplane as a weapon although it had been used as one before. On December 7, 1941, an enemy that used airplanes in the same manner attacked the United States. It took about a generation to go from peak to peak of our expectations of safety.

The past is full of outcomes that look quite obvious today. Without the ability to step back from the situation and measure their expectations, there will always be missed outcomes.

Future events are the most beneficial to predict, and we can use the past to help identify their natural limits. The outcomes to events in the past are what we must research to determine the natural limits of the event.

In the case of the current financial crisis, we understand that in the past an over extension of credit results in the same outcome which is deflation. At the end of credit-driven economic growth, credit is easier to obtain than ever before. Creditors take on more risk, and investors demand more return. These perfect series of events in the past have led to The Great Depression, Tulip Mania, The Mississippi Bubble, The South Sea Bubble, etc. All of the aforementioned events shared the same outcome of deflation. Over extension of credit creates inflation. When we look back to the early 1980s, rates on mortgages were over 15 percent; $100,000 financed then is the equivalent of $225,000 today with mortgage rates around 5 percent. What we pay for credit is directly related to the Federal Funds Rate – the higher the rate the less banks lend; the lower the rate the more they lend. The Federal Funds Rate was over 18 percent in 1982; today, as of this writing, it is 0 to .25 percent (target rate). Inflation over the past 30 years has been masked by credit. The Federal Reserve has lowered rates to reverse the effects of recessions that occurred during this time frame. It is fair to say they have lowered rates more than raised them. With the overnight bank rate at 0 to .25 percent, the amount of credit available is at its natural limit. At this point it is not a predictable but logical outcome. The quality of credit will start to deteriorate as it did in the past. As

103

outstanding loans default, the money supply shrinks and so does the available credit. These actions directly cause deflation which creates a depression.

History repeats itself, and scholars look back to determine what they believe could have prevented the event. Since most scholars do not consider these events are caused by human instincts, their conclusions are subjective and typically cause more harm than good especially if one of these scholars directly influences the actions of the Federal Reserve in the future.

6

The Simple Stock Market Expectations Indicator

We have discussed thoroughly who we are and why we do what we do. To this point we have only discussed theoretical ways to predict personal and group action outcomes. As mentioned before "hind sight is twenty-twenty" and the conclusions in this book are not conceived from a study of why certain outcomes occur. The theories presented here are rather the result of an experiment that has had significant success in predicting stock market changes. The theories discussed so far have been to explain why it has worked rather than how it works. This indicator was stumbled upon and developed. The general expectations theory was present at the birth of the indicator, but it was only in the evaluation and research into the results did the details emerge.

We will discuss how to measure and interpret expectations of the Dow Jones Industrial Average Index. We will discuss what the natural limits are and how they were determined. We will look at the results over time evaluating its successes as well as its failures. We will see how this indicator gives us a more logical explanation to why the index goes up and down then current beliefs.

6.1 Why the Dow Jones Industrial Average?

Why out of all the possible indexes are we measuring expectations on the Dow Jones Industrial Average? Simply, the Dow is a good representation of industry in the United States with the fewest moving parts. We could measure the S&P 500, but we would be measuring 500 stocks on a daily basis rather than just the 30 in the Dow. We need to keep the process simple and easy to calculate. Fewer moving parts leave less open to interpretation. The Dow Jones Industrial Average also has the power to move the market as a whole. If 3M (a Dow component as of this writing) is down on high expectations, it is more likely its peers will respond sympathetically. It is extremely rare to see the Dow Jones Industrial Average up without the S&P 500 up or vice versa. Many Wall Street professionals view the S&P 500 as the real measurement of the overall stock market, but their movements over time have almost always corresponded. See figure 6.1.

There are many ways to trade the Dow Jones Industrial Average through futures, Exchange Traded Funds, Mutual Funds, or even the individual stocks in the index. By investing in an index over individual stocks, we minimize the risk of random events that can occur with the individual companies.

So we have established that the Dow 30 is easier to track than the S&P 500 because of the sheer number of stocks to follow. We understand that although the returns between the averages can be different the direction of the movement almost always corresponds and becomes more linear over time. We also have determined that our predictions are actionable and scalable because of the numerous ways to trade the average.

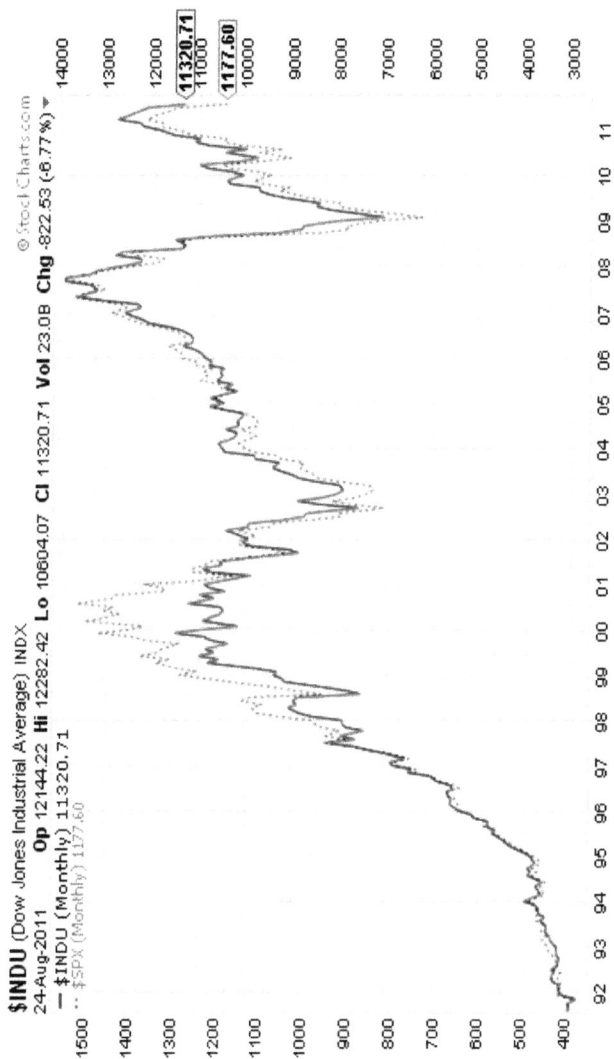

Figure 6.1 DJIA vs S&P 500 over 20 year period

This indicator helps determine the path of least resistance for the DJIA. We will also discuss ways to select sectors within the market that may outperform the average based off its expectations in relation to other sectors.

When one market goes up another typically goes down. If we determine that expectations are high and we are bearish on the DJIA, we would look for the treasury market to be bullish. There are many correlations between equities and other investments. Some of these correlations are temporary and others are a seesaw effect, if one goes up the other goes down. Over the past decade it has become commonly accepted that stocks have moved in correlation with commodities. This correlation typically means that a bull market currently depends on a weak US Dollar. We will discuss different ways to interoperate this data, but I will not attempt to explain the mechanics of different trading systems since we must be in full understanding of a market before we invest in it. If we do not understand why the US Dollar going down in value results in commodities prices going up, then we should not attempt to take advantage of this current correlation.

6.2 Keeping Track of the Dow's expectations

The DJIA is made up of 30 stocks that are meant to reflect the United States industrial sector. The Dow Jones company attempts to represent every industry including Consumer Goods, Basic Materials, Energy, Healthcare, Technology, Financial Services, and Industrial Goods. The stocks that represent these industries can change at the discretion of the Dow Jones Company. Since these stocks can change (such as Citigroup was recently removed due to their share price slipping to low single digits in early 2009 and GM was also removed for rather obvious reasons), we must continually check for changes to the index.

Each of these stocks that make up the DJIA carries a different weight in the average, but since this weighting is continuously changing, we will not take it into consideration. In the early development of this indicator, I attempted to take the different weightings into consideration but found the data complicated the results and was no more and actually less accurate than just counting each stock the same.

As discussed earlier in "Measuring Expectations," we only measure an expectation that is readily available and gives us an actionable outcome with either a yes or no answer. The data must not be open to interpretation and common among its peers. The only readily available information in stock expectations that meets this criterion is their earnings expectations from one day to the next. Earnings expectations for individual stocks are set by both the issuing company and analysts from banks, brokerages, and independent groups. This information

111

represents their optimism or pessimism from day to day. We understand from previous discussions that as optimism mounts so do expectations and vice versa as pessimism increases.

To track this data we must create a spreadsheet. On the left of the sheet we list the stock symbols of the DJIA 30 stocks. On the top of each column we list the dates of the data collected. Keep in mind that since this data is available daily we should be listing every day from today forward. Since DJIA stocks only trade Monday through Friday, excluding holidays, our spreadsheet should reflect only these dates.

After creating a place to record our data, we are ready to start gathering it. It is prudent to gather this data before the market opens. This information is readily available on the Internet. As of this writing, Yahoo Finance has this information easily accessible without cost. First, we enter the stock symbol to obtain a quote. On the quote page we click on the "Analysts Estimates" tab currently on the middle left of the screen. As we view the Analysts Estimates, we are only interested in one piece of information from the slew of numbers that appear. The analysts' estimates for a stock's current quarter's earnings change from today to seven days ago, 30 days ago, 60 days ago, and 90 days ago. We are only interested in the change from seven days ago. The reason we are looking at only the seven-day period is because we are recording a daily view of expectations. By looking at this information, we identify when earnings expectations are raised or lowered for each of these stocks by the groups that control these expectations. After retrieving this information, we record it accurately onto our spreadsheet. As discussed earlier we apply a value for each event. If the expectations have gone up from 7 days ago to today, then we would record a value of 1 on our spreadsheet matching the date and symbol. If the earnings expectations have gone down from 7 days ago to today, then we would record a value of -1 on our spreadsheet again matching date with symbol. If earnings are unchanged, then we would record a value of 0. After gathering this information on all 30 Dow components, we would calculate the sum of all of these values for that day to determine the expectations. See figure 6.2 for an example.

The process of gathering this information becomes easier as we begin to memorize the symbols and get use to the method of recording expectations of the DJIA. We must pay attention to changes in the index so we continue to measure the correct stocks, as mentioned earlier.

Although it is not necessary, we could chart the daily expectations. By charting the daily DJIA expectations, it makes it easier to recognize the natural limit.

Determining the natural limit of these daily expectations takes several cycles of high and low expectation moves to realize them. Since these expectations have been tracked for more than a year, the natural limit has already been determined. Keep in mind that this step of determining natural limits is extremely important if we expect to predict outcomes accurately. The more data we amass the more refined the prediction becomes.

Dow 30	7/19/10	7/20/10
mmm	1	1
aa	-1	-1
axp	1	1
t	0	0
bac	0	-1
ba	-1	-1
cat	1	1
cvx	1	1
trv	0	0
dd	0	0
xom	-1	0
ge	0	0
csco	0	0
hpq	0	0
intc	1	1
ibm	0	0
jnj	0	0
jpm	1	1
kft	0	0
mcd	0	0
mrk	0	0
msft	0	-1
pfe	0	0
ko	0	0
hd	1	1
pg	0	0
utx	0	-1
vz	0	0
wmt	0	0
dis	0	0
total	4	2

Figure 6.2 Example Expectations Spreadsheet

6.3 The Dow's Natural Limits

As we discussed earlier with expectations, before they can turn they must touch their limits. These limits are the point where they can no longer go higher or lower.

Using this information to predict outcomes does not have value until we establish at what point expectations have peaked or bottomed. This is the point where the group or person has straight A's, and no matter what they do, they cannot exceed their expectations since it is impossible to go any higher.

Since tracking the daily expectations of the DJIA over a year, we have determined its natural limit. The natural limits exist at a plus 7 and minus 7. Keep in mind that we must determine the direction of expectations before acting on them. If we record a value of five when we first start, until we record a value of seven or minus seven we are unable to determine where expectations currently are. When we get a reading of a plus 7, we assume that the DJIA has reached its high expectations limit, and it needs to touch a minus 7 to change its direction again.

A reading of a plus 7 on expectations tells us that the market has gotten ahead of actual events, and it is more likely to fail then succeed. During this high expectations time period we see stocks exceed listed expected earnings and still sell because the market already has high expectations. A common Wall Street expression refers to this as "buy the rumor, sell the news." We understand based off of previous discussions that even if expectations turn to a negative number they must touch minus 7 in order to change the direction of expectations; a high is met with an equal low.

A minus 7 expectations on the DJIA signals a bottom in expectations and results in stocks exceeding expectations more than missing. Again, during this period of low expectations we could see companies miss listed expectations but still go higher in trading because the market has low expectations.

Expectations continue to cycle from high to low over and over again. Markets move within different cycles. It is possible to have a bull market cycle within a longer bear market cycle and vice versa. Even though a market may have low expectations, therefore bullish, long term the market may be generally bearish. Only over time do we see this long-term pattern occur. For a market to be long term, bullish highs exceed lows, and during a bear, market lows exceed highs.

Since the inception of this indicator, it has been quite accurate in taking advantage of both the highs and the lows. To truly take full advantage of any market place, we must be willing to play on both sides of the court. In the following section, we will discuss ways to use this information to our benefit.

6.4 Using the Stock Market Expectations Indicator

From our previous discussions, the obvious way to use this information about the expectations of the Dow Industrial Average would to go long (buy) the Dow Industrial Average when expectations are low and sell when they are high.

It is very important we understand that expectations only change when they touch their natural limits. For example, if the daily expectations' values resulted in the following:

Day 1: 7 (expectations value for that day)
Day 2: 5
Day 3: 6
Day 4: 2
Day 5: -3
Day 6: -2
Day 7: -5
Day 8: 1
Day 9: -6
Day 10: -7

We would have a bear biased on Day one and would only change our direction when expectations touched -7 on "Day 10," and at this point we would go to a bull stance. Although in the above example expectations turned negative on "Day 3," the cycle must be completed for the momentum to change. This has been discussed at length and must be adhered to for the indicator to demonstrate its effectiveness. The most difficult part of using this indicator is the patience it requires. Sometimes expectations can change in weeks and other times it takes months. We must ignore the market's daily fluctuations and focus on the end results. The market will go up and down during these periods. The indicator is used to help identify whether it will go up more than down or vice versa. Markets never move in straight lines.

Another very important item we must understand is the current relationships between markets. There are temporary relationships and historic ones. To utilize this indicator correctly we must take the time to identify what these temporary and historic relationships are.

As discussed earlier, historically, when the stock market goes down the treasury market goes up, and vice versa, when the market goes up the treasury market goes down. The concept behind this relationship is when the market is under pressure investors buy United States Treasuries for shelter, and they sell them when the market is going up to raise money to invest. We must keep in mind that with any relationship it can be temporary.

A temporary relationship between markets currently exists (again previously discussed) between the value of the US Dollar and the Stock Market. When the Dollar is strong, the market is weak, and vice versa, when it is weak the Market is strong. Since the US Dollar index is how it compares to a basket of currencies, a better measurement of the dollar strength is with the value of commodities. When commodities' prices are up, especially in oil, the dollar is weak. The opposite holds true when they are under pressure, the dollar is strong. We will not thoroughly discuss why commodities reflect the strength of the US Dollar, but it is commonly accepted because commodities around the world are priced in the US Dollars. See figure 6.3.

When we change our bias, it is important to know how to benefit from the information. As we discussed before, we can use various investment vehicles to capitalize on the effectiveness of this indicator. The investment tools we use really depend on the risk we are able to take. Determining risk tolerance will not be a part of our discussion; this is up to us, or our accountant, or any other financial professional we rely on who is intimately aware of our financial health. As said before the obvious method is to buy when there are low expectations and sell when there are high expectations. There are other ways to benefit from this information on either side of the risk spectrum. There are many different tools to be a bull on the market or a bear, as discussed already, which could include mutual funds, Exchange Traded Funds, Futures, Bonds, Treasuries, etc. Everyday Wall Street comes up with new ways we can take a bull or bear position; it is up to us to determine the best product that matches our risk tolerance with product knowledge.

The Art of Expectations

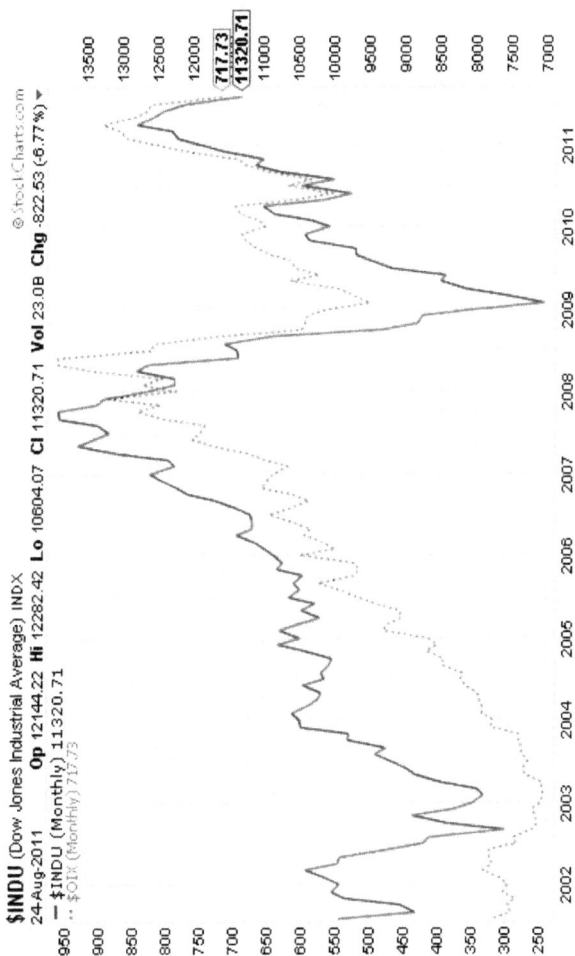

$INDU (Dow Jones Industrial Average) INDX
24-Aug-2011   Op 12144.22 Hi 12282.42 Lo 10604.07 Cl 11320.71 Vol 23.0B Chg -822.53 (-6.77%) ▼
— $INDU (Monthly) 11320.71
∷ $OIX (Monthly) 717.73

Figure 6.3 DJIA vs CBOE Oil Index

The Art of Expectations

6.5 The Track Record

As the saying goes "the proof is in the pudding." As with any indicator or tool like the one we have discussed here, it works until it no longer works. The indicator we have discussed carries no guarantees of accuracy in the future, but in the past it has been very accurate. We will take a look at the accuracy of the indicator over a period of over a year and let the results speak for themselves.

First, we will review the days over the year where expectations hit their limits and then compare them to the Dow Jones Industrial Average. See figure 6.4.

The following are the dates when expectations changed:

June 8, 2009 – Expectations recorded at 7 signaling high expectations resulting in a bearish bias.

July 13, 2009 – Expectations were recorded at -7 signaling low expectations and changing bear bias to bull.

September 28, 2009 – Expectations were recorded at 7 signaling high expectations and a bear environment. This is the only recorded expectations change that did not mark a market move. Even though the market did not change in the expectations' favor, it did not move substantially in any direction when compared to the next change.

February 4, 2010 – Expectations were recorded at a value of -7 signaling low expectations changing our bias from bear to bull.

April 23, 2010 – Expectations were recorded at 7 signaling high expectations moving us from bullish to bearish.

October 18, 2010 – Expectations were recorded at 8. This is a sign of an expectations' abnormality, which will be discussed in the next chapter. This retest in high expectations has marked the beginning of a bubble in the markets. Until the market breaks, this level it will trade outside of real expectations, which is a sign of delusion. This delusion was caused more likely by the actions of the US Federal Reserve when in August they announced *quantitative easing two*, which proved unsuccessful, in hopes to manipulate the markets to take on more risk.

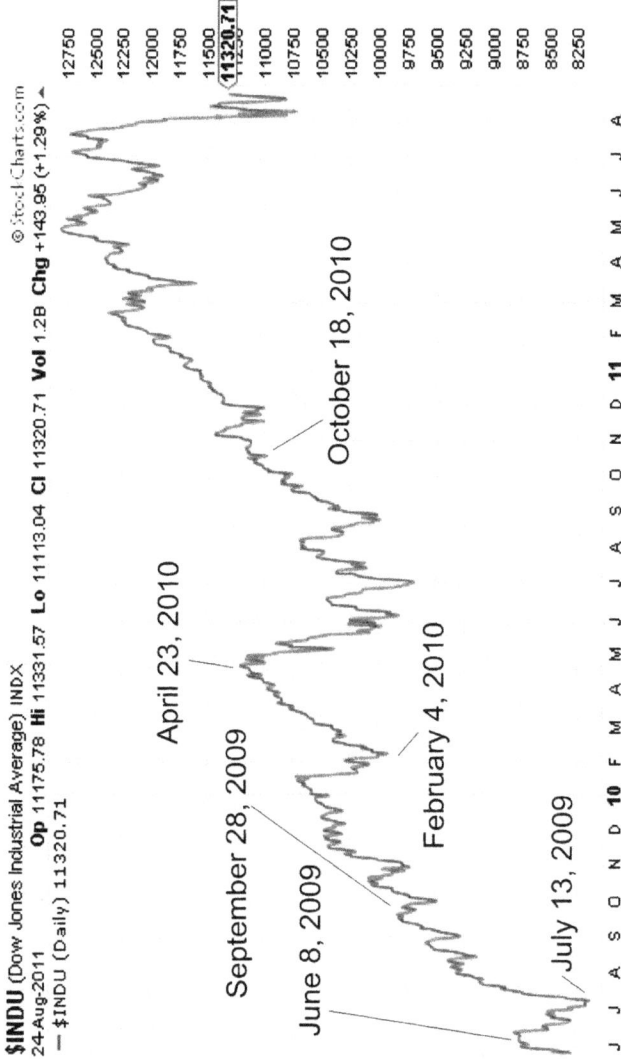

$INDU (Dow Jones Industrial Average) INDX
24-Aug-2011   Op 11175.78 Hi 11331.57 Lo 11113.04 Cl 11320.71 Vol 1.2B Chg +143.95 (+1.29%) ▲
— $INDU (Daily) 11320.71

© StockCharts.com

11320.71

September 28, 2009

April 23, 2010

October 18, 2010

June 8, 2009

February 4, 2010

July 13, 2009

Figure 6.4 Chart of DJIA from May 26, 2009 till August 23, 2011

Now we compare expectations changes to market data. Again see figure 6.4 that illustrates the effectiveness of this "Simple Stock Market Expectation Indicator." To illustrate the point in time when expectations changed, I have noted these dates on the charts.

As from the charts, we can see the expectations indicator has been very accurate in pinpointing momentum changes in the market. We can see expectations managed to take advantage of both of the bull and bear moves.

As already said this method of gauging the expectations of the Dow Jones Industrial Average has proven accurate, but the future of its accuracy is unpredictable. The future could be swayed by politics, corruption or access to data. We must with any form of investing continuously evaluate its effectiveness.

7

Expectation's Abnormalities

As discussed at length, expectations are a result of our instincts or as detailed before as our "Normal Attributes." Instincts, as with animals, are meant to protect and preserve our way of life. Without these instincts that define who and what we are our lives would lack control and structure. Expectations cycles are natural, and the highs and lows are required to allow us to move forward. If a high is prevented from meeting its natural low, our cycle is disrupted, and our lives become unnatural until the disruption is dislodged.

Abnormal expectations cycles are more of a disruption in the process than an actual abnormality. They may cause abnormal durations in the completion of a cycle, since typically a low comes much faster than the high it precedes, but rest assured nature always wins over manipulation.

What truly defines the difference between a low and a high expectation is the margin of error at either end. When we are at the beginning of building expectations, our margin of error is very large; we have room to make mistakes, therefore, making our possibility of success more likely. As we approach our peak of expectations, the margin for error is very small, therefore, making it harder and harder to succeed. When we hit the peak of expectations, there is no other possible outcome but failure. Sometimes this failure point is sustained for a long period of time especially if the ascent in expectations has lasted for a long period of time. The longer we ascended in expectations the harder it is for us to let go. We cling to hope for a return back to the good times and "stay off" the impending descent.

This attempt to "stay off" this natural force, which is imbedded in our DNA as human beings, creates an abnormal environment. This environment is best described as a form of limbo. We are neither moving forward or backwards, but damage is being done. The longer we fight nature, the more violent the descent becomes. These periods of time are identifiable. Staying objective and removed from the action or event makes these abnormal behaviors obvious.

Everyday we identify this "limbo" in our friends and family. It is easy to see a person who we have regular contact with, who is not willing to let go of the past, and is unwilling to acknowledge that they have met their limit. Unfortunately, we spend a lot of our time on the other end of this observation as the victim rather than a casual observer. Most of the time we are just unaware members of a larger ship (group), which is sinking.

So, how do we identify this abnormal stage in an expectations cycle? The easiest way to see through this deception is to adopt a concept already detailed earlier.

"Look for the bad news in the good and the good in the bad."

If everyone is feeling the glass is half full, maybe it is time to look at it half empty for a change. This concept may just sound contrarian, and it is to an extent. Unfortunately, sometimes being contrarian is the very thing we must challenge. Another obvious sign of this limbo can be seen when reactions to missed expectations are ignored. This typically is the result of a large group peaking in expectations and hoping for a return to normalcy. Unfortunately, the "new normal" is actually missed expectations and a large descent.

An example of this view existed recently on a broad scale with the real estate bubble bursting. Before the real estate bubble popped, the signs were obvious if we did not have a vested interest in it. The most obvious sign was the conforming loan limits, which defines a mortgage as a standard loan or a jumbo. This limit nearly doubled in less than 10 years. Residential real estate for hundreds of years has always been, and time has proven, an inflation hedge rather than an investment growth tool. Also, as an observer rather than a participant we would have noticed that mortgage payments were staying low, but values were accelerating at an unsustainable pace. An objective view of the real estate market would have easily identified an abnormal growth pace.

If we are participating in the deception, the hardest thing to do is to really have an objective view. A relatively simple way to realize whether we are involved in an abnormal stage of an expectations' cycle is to apply basic logic to our beliefs and our actions. When we act or believe in a concept, we convince ourselves of the truth in it. Look at these truths, and apply basic logic to them. Typically, this abnormal stage is the concept or belief that preoccupies the majority of our thoughts and actions. Logic should be defined by historic truths. We understand that real estate does not double in less than 10 years so, therefore, we understand that it is abnormal.

This abnormal stage, or limbo, does not just exist at a peak of an expectations cycle being met. It also can occur at an extreme low. Typically this "limbo" at the bottom precedes the stall at the top. The damage can be equally destructive. Expectations limits at either end of the spectrum are equally damaging.

No matter how long this abnormal stall in the natural cycle of expectations occurs, nature always wins. Our patience and confidence in this concept will be tested during this stage, but our objective and removed logical view will eventually prevail.

7.1 The Future According to Current Expectations

According to the Expectations Indicator all signs point to an Expectations Abnormality. The current stock and commodities market action of late is probably the most destructive stall at the top of expectation in the past 100 years. The delusion of growth and prosperity has been at the expense of the average citizen. This stall was actually formulated artificially by Government officials around the world and, therefore, is unnatural. Just as with artificial groups, the end result is more erratic and violent. Eventually, nature will prevail since we are just human.

We are on the edge of a large descent of expectations. All market news regardless of whether it missed expectations is viewed as a positive. The financial news is full of hope rather than current events. This current event will more likely be viewed as the Great Deception of the 21st Century rather than the great recovery.

As with all expectations, the descent will be painful. We will take a long time to let go of our current normal and adopt the new one. Although the near future is rather bleak, out of all falling expectations comes a bottom and then another ascent. In the future the near term bottom will be credited to the following ascent. These expectations bottoms highlight our destructive instincts and allow us to suppress them until we forget again. As history has shown us, unfortunately we will repeat our errors probably a generation away.

The Art of Expectations